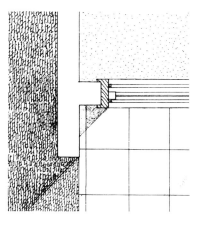

ARCHITECTURAL ILLUSTRATION
INSIDE AND OUT

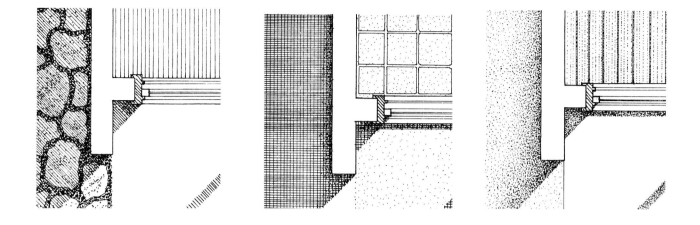

ARCHITECTURAL ILLUSTRATION
INSIDE AND OUT

Albert Lorenz and Leonard Lizak

WHITNEY LIBRARY OF DESIGN
An imprint of Watson-Guptill Publications/New York

Acknowledgments

Tony Ianniciello
Chris Clay
Ron Hoina
Curtis Wagner
Michael Flynn
Kirsten Lorenz
Maureen Lorenz
Joy Schleh
Christian Xatrec

A Read/Write Publication
First published in New York by Whitney Library of Design
an imprint of Watson-Guptill Publications
a division of Billboard Publications, Inc.
1515 Broadway, New York, NY 10036

Library of Congress Cataloging-in-Publication Data

Lorenz, Albert, 1941–
    Architectural illustration inside and out / by Albert
Lorenz and Leonard Lizak.
        p.   cm.
        Bibliography: p.
        Includes index.
        ISBN 0-8230-0244-6   ISBN 0-8230-0246-2 (pbk.)
        1. Architectural drawing—Technique.   2. Architectural rendering—
Technique.   3. Architectural drawing—Detailing—Technique.
4. Interior decoration rendering—Technique. I. Lizak, Leonard.
II. Title.
NA2708.L67 1988
720'.28' 4—dc19   88-17308
                                                    C I P

Manufactured in U.S.A.

First printing, 1988

1 2 3 4 5 6 7 8 9 / 93 92 91 90 89 88

To our parents

CONTENTS

INTRODUCTION

The only way to learn drawing is to draw. A book that is intended to teach drawing skills and techniques *must be visual*. It must show examples, so that the user understands what he or she is working toward. People who look at a book on drawing rarely read it; they look at the pictures. This book is designed to capitalize on that fact. Drawings and photographs take the place of words, providing images to copy and to emulate.

Use this book as you would any reference book. Look through it; familiarize yourself with its contents. When you are working on a drawing, use the visual examples to help you put your own drawing together.

Drawing is a mental and physical skill. Anyone can draw, and draw competently, but you must work at it. Practice is essential. To repeat: the only way to learn drawing is to draw.

In order to draw, of course, you need certain basic skills. The purpose of this book is to put these skills at your fingertips.

For a beginner, visualization is difficult. This book explains technique in the simplest of terms, but more importantly, it gives you many visual examples. Use them as a guide to draw—and draw! You can actually teach yourself

Begin with the drafting basics and practice for at least two weeks. Then set up a project for yourself. Design a house for an imaginary client. Draft the site plan, floor plans, elevations, and sections. Keep them simple. Then delineate all the construction materials, the furnishings and the surroundings, the light and shadow. Give yourself a week to do the project. When you have finished, put it aside. You are ready for another project.

Next, pick something slightly more difficult. Illustrate someone else's design, perhaps something you have seen in a magazine or drawings you can borrow from a fellow student or a friend who is an architect or interior designer. Even though the drawings already exist, redraw them in your own way using your new skills.

When this set of drawings is finished, compare them with your first project. Criticize them. What is good about them? How could they be better? What are the weak points?

Your third project should be the most complex. Time yourself; this project should take less time than the first two. As you continue learning, not only will you get better, but you will get faster. Move on to more complex techniques and projects. You are on your way to becoming a true professional, confident and skilled. Keep practicing.

Chapter 1: THE BASICS

If you intend to do a lot of drawing, you should set up a space just for your work. Your studio may be a room, or it may be a corner of a room, but the minimum you need is a place to put a worktable. This is where you will do all your drawing. Use a sturdy table that is at least 30 by 40 inches in size. The table should be normal height (30 inches, approximately), so that when you sit in your chair your feet are touching the ground. This is important, since you will spend many hours at your table and you should be as comfortable as possible.

You will also need a chair, the most comfortable you can afford. Be sure it provides back support.

Also get the best light because your eyes are so important to you. A combination light with a regular incandescent light bulb and a fluorescent tube is best. You can purchase a combination light in any art-supply store. They are expensive, but worth the outlay.

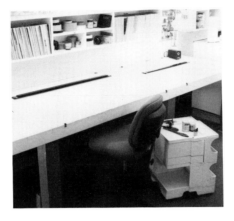

Materials

You will need the following supplies, all available in art-supply stores, before you can start work.

A *board (table) cover* to cover your drawing surface. It should be a material that has a little give, such as a vinyl or rubber pad. Never draw on glass or wood. These surfaces are unyielding and your paper will tear.

A *parallel*, so you can draw parallel horizontal lines. A parallel also acts as a base for your

triangles. The 42-inch parallel, the smallest size that still allows you to work on 30-by-40-inch board or paper, is recommended. Don't bother to buy a T-square; this is outdated as a drawing tool.

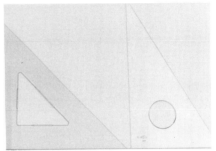

Three *triangles* (30, 60, and 45 degrees) and a *small, adjustable triangle.* Make sure they are all clear plastic and have right-angle edges. Never use your triangle for cutting.

A *steel ruler*, the tool to use for cutting. This is the *only* tool to use for cutting straight lines; never use your triangles or your parallel because you can nick the plastic edges, ruining them for drawing straight lines.

Drawing pencils, wood or mechanical. They are really the

same in quality. The choice is just a matter of personal preference. You can purchase an automatic or manual sharpener for either type pencil.

All pencils have a number and a letter designation. B is soft; H is hard. The higher the number, the softer or harder the lead will be. So 6B is much softer than 2B, and 6H is harder than 2H.

A *manual* or *automatic eraser.* The difference, as with most drafting equipment, is cost. An electric eraser is, of course, much more expensive than a manual one, but it does a faster, more thorough job.

You can erase both pencil and ink, but you must use the correct eraser for each medium. In other words, to erase ink, use an ink eraser; to erase pencil, use a pencil eraser. White plastic erasers are good because they don't affect the color or the surface of the board you are working on.

An *erasing shield* for small areas. It will keep you from erasing parts of the drawing that should not be touched.

Masking tape or *drafting tape* for taping a drawing to your drawing table. Never use clear tape, the kind used for wrapping packages, because the tape will tear the surface of your drawing when you try to remove it. Masking tape and drafting tape are the *only* kinds of tape that will not damage the surface on which you are drawing.

An *architectural scale.* Usually 12 inches long, it has various scales on it that are used in doing architectural drawing. You must choose a scale for each drawing you do and clearly indicate the scale on the drawing by showing it visually.

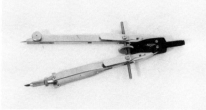

A *compass,* which is indispensable yet not expensive. Get one that has an inking attachment so that you can use it for either pen or pencil lines.

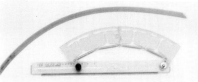

An *adjustable curve* for drawing large, gentle curves. Choose

plastic rather than the black rubber type. The plastic curve holds its shape better.

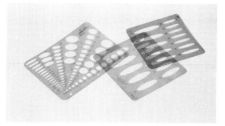

French curves for drawing precise curves. Available in various shapes and sizes, these plastic templates are used to draw circles, ellipses, and other geometric shapes, and as an aid in lettering.

Knives for cutting paper, cardboard, and wood. They come in various shapes and sizes. The heavier the blade, the heavier the cut the blade will make.

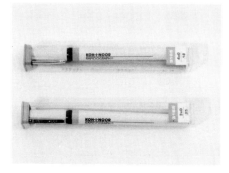

Technical pens such as the Rapidograph. Although available in varying point sizes from 000000 (the smallest point) to 4 (the thickest), the range from 0000 to 1 is the most useful. The makers of most technical pens advise you to use the brand of ink they manufacture. The ink has additives to make it flow easily through the pen. Try different brands and use the one that you like; just make sure that it is black and waterproof.

Skum-X to sprinkle on your drawing to keep it clean. The small, soft particles in this product form a light barrier between the drawing and the parallel and triangles that travel over it. This barrier keeps the parallel and triangles from smudging your pencil line.

To keep your drawing clean, also use a **drafting brush** to sweep dirt, dust, and erasure crumbs off the drawing surface; otherwise these materials become ground into the drawing's surface and are impossible to remove completely.

Several types of **tracing paper**, ranging from the highest quality to the cheapest. Thumbnail tracing paper comes in yellow and white and is the cheapest tracing paper you can use. It tears easily, so use pencil only and erase carefully. This paper should be used only for overlays, not for finished drawings.

Vellum tracing paper, which can be purchased in rolls or pads, is slightly more expensive than thumbnail and should be used in the same way.

One-hundred-percent rag tracing paper is the most expensive and should be used only for finished drawings. To find the brand and type that suit you best, you must experiment. You

must prepare rag tracing paper before you use ink on it. To prepare it, you must rub in a product called pounce, then brush the excess off the surface of the paper. This powder does not keep the drawing clean; rather, it prepares the surface to receive ink. If you do not rub in pounce, the ink will not adhere to the paper and will be erasable.

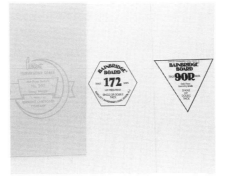

Illustration board in various thicknesses and surface textures. At times you will need a sturdier surface than tracing paper for your drawing. This is when you will use illustration board. Pick the thickness and texture that best suit your job. If you draw with a wet medium, you must use a board that will not warp and will absorb the water. If you use pencil, the texture of the board should be compatible.

Pencil sharpeners, either electric or manual. The choice is yours; the difference is price and speed.

Rubber cement, rubber cement thinner, and **fixatif.** These are essential tools. Rubber cement is used to glue paper to paper and can be unglued with rubber cement thinner. Fixatif protects any pencil work, color or regular. Once sprayed with fixatif the pencil drawing will not smudge.

A **roller ruler.** This is a simple tool that works well when you have to draw a series of parallel lines. Draw the first line and then roll the ruler down or up and draw the subsequent lines; all will be parallel to the first.

Lupes. These little magnifiers are used to see the details of a slide or transparency without the use of a projector. Using a lupe provides a way to use a slide as a reference since you can look at the details and draw without having to set up a projector and keep it running.

Drafting Techniques

The following photographs and text will show you how to use some of the materials discussed. With practice, using each tool will become second nature.

The angle of your pen or pencil must always be the same. Keep the point away from the triangle or parallel.

Keep your pencil line even and dark; as you draw, rotate the pencil slightly. This will keep the line sharp and thin and reduce the number of times needed to sharpen your pencil. How many lines can you draw before you need to sharpen your pencil? This is an individual thing, depending on how hard you press down and your ability to rotate the pencil.

Each pen has a different thickness.

Erasing by hand is relatively easy. Use a plastic eraser and an erasing shield.

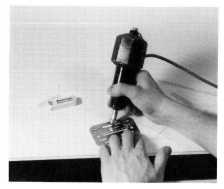

Erasing with an electric eraser is also simple. Remember to use the appropriate eraser (ink or plastic) and an erasing shield. Be careful not to erase through whatever surface you are working on. Always test your eraser on a scrap of the same paper you are using before working on the final drawing.

When inking, always pull the line toward or away from you; never push it. Use the same angle with your triangles and parallel that you would use when delineating in pencil. Keep the pressure on your pen constant. Your line must be the same thickness throughout, whether it is drawn freehand or with a straightedge.

It is very important to keep your pens clean. They clog very easily.

Become adept at taking your pens apart and putting them together again. Here is a simple step-by-step guide.

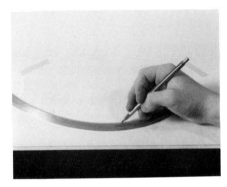

Use your adjustable curves, French curves, and templates as you need them. There is really nothing difficult or special about them. The question is not *how to* but *when*.

When drawing, rest your arms on a towel, not on your drawing. Use these towels as a way to keep dirt off your drawing and also as a cushion for your forearm.

For finished drawings always use

one-hundred-percent rag tracing paper, which must be prepared before you can ink on it. To prepare this paper, rub in pounce and then brush it away. Now the ink will adhere to the paper.

Always sketch a curve freehand before you use a template. The feeling of a freehand drawing is altogether different from a straightedge drawing. The straightedge line is precise and machinelike. The freehand line is loose and informal.

When drawing a line, never draw in the shadow of your triangle. Make sure the light source is on the other side of the triangle. Pull the pencil or pen away from you or pull it toward you, *never* push it.

Always cut using a steel ruler as a guide. When cutting, apply

pressure with the knife in the area between the fingers and thumb of your holding hand. Never carry the knife past this area. To cut further, move your holding hand. You should always cut with your hand on the steel ruler opposite the knife.

A transparency of your subject matter is helpful for checking details while drawing. It can be used with a lupe if you need to see minute details.

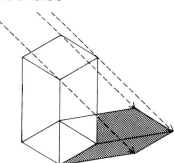
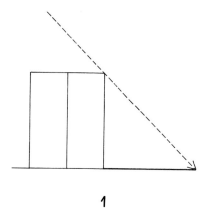
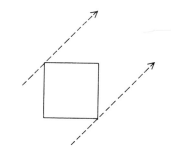

1

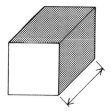
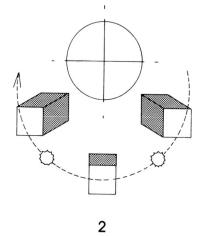
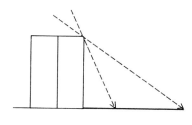

2

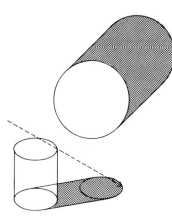
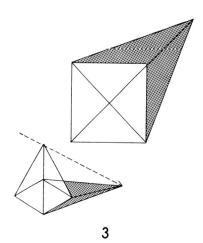
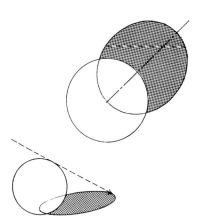

3

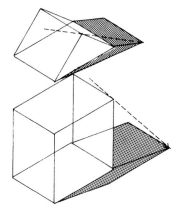
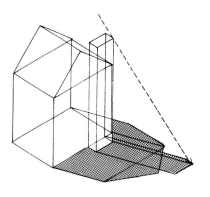
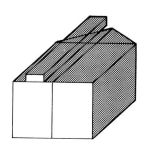

4

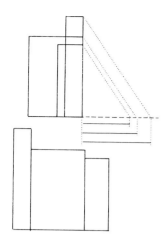

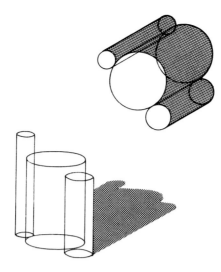

5

LIGHT

Without a light source, it is difficult to understand a drawing. A piece of architecture unmodulated by light and shadow is flat, and the relationship of its parts are unclear.

1. Several variables affect an object that casts a shadow on the ground. First is the angle of the sun with respect to the ground.

2. Second is the direction of the sun with respect to the object. The angle of the sun is what determines the length of the shadow. The direction from which the sun comes tells exactly where the shadow will fall.

3 and **4.** These variables combine to produce a shadow of a particular size and shape.

5. This illustration is a more complicated shape, showing the shadow as constructed in plan and elevation.

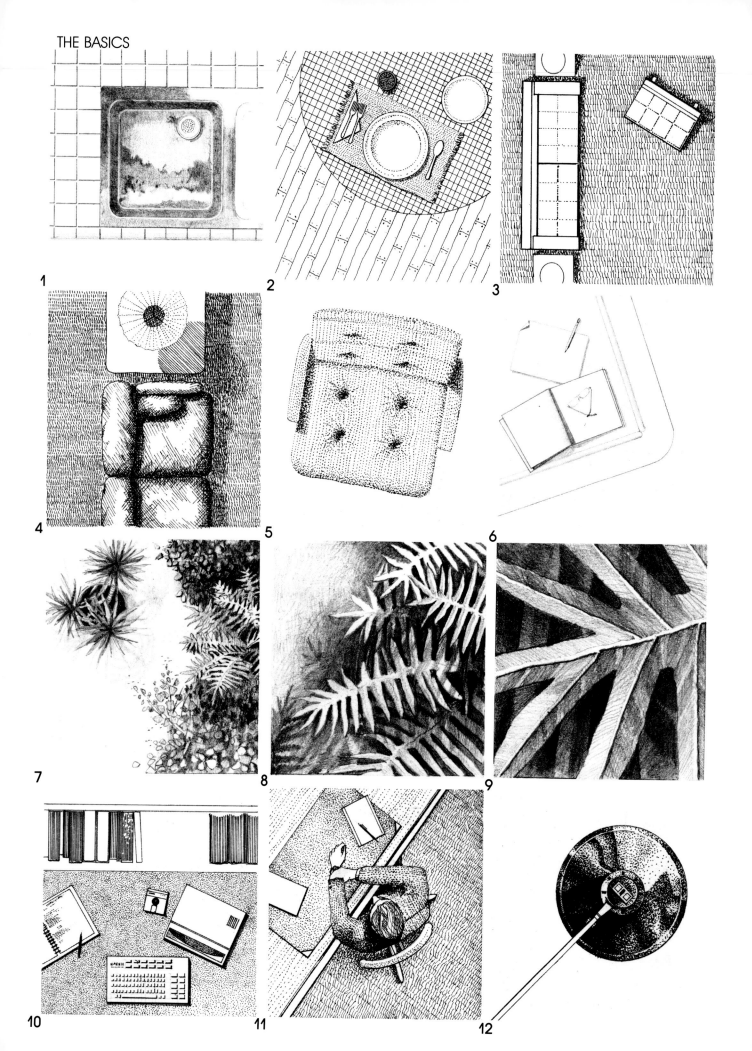

1

2

3

4

5

6

7

8

9

10

11

12

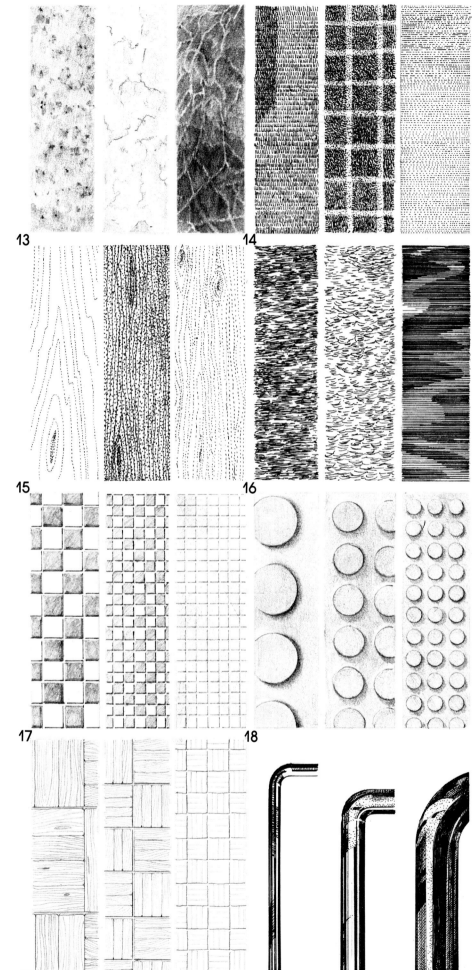

13

14

15

16

17

18

19

20

TEXTURES

Learning to draw textures takes imagination and practice, but mastering this ability will be worth all the effort you put into it. Texture is the lifeblood of your drawing. It makes it come alive. Texture adds depth and can give an almost tactile quality to what you illustrate. There is no limit to the variations that you can create when delineating different surfaces. Here are samples to imitate. After you have mastered these, create other textures of your own.

Interior Textures

1.	Kitchen sink
2.	Table setting
3.	Couch, chair, rug
4.	Leather couch
5.	Fabric-covered chair
6.	Desktop
7–9.	Leaves
10.	Desktop
11.	Man at work
12.	Lamp
13.	Marble
14.	Rug
15.	Wood
16.	Water
17.	Tiles
18.	Rubber flooring
19.	Parquet floor
20.	Chrome

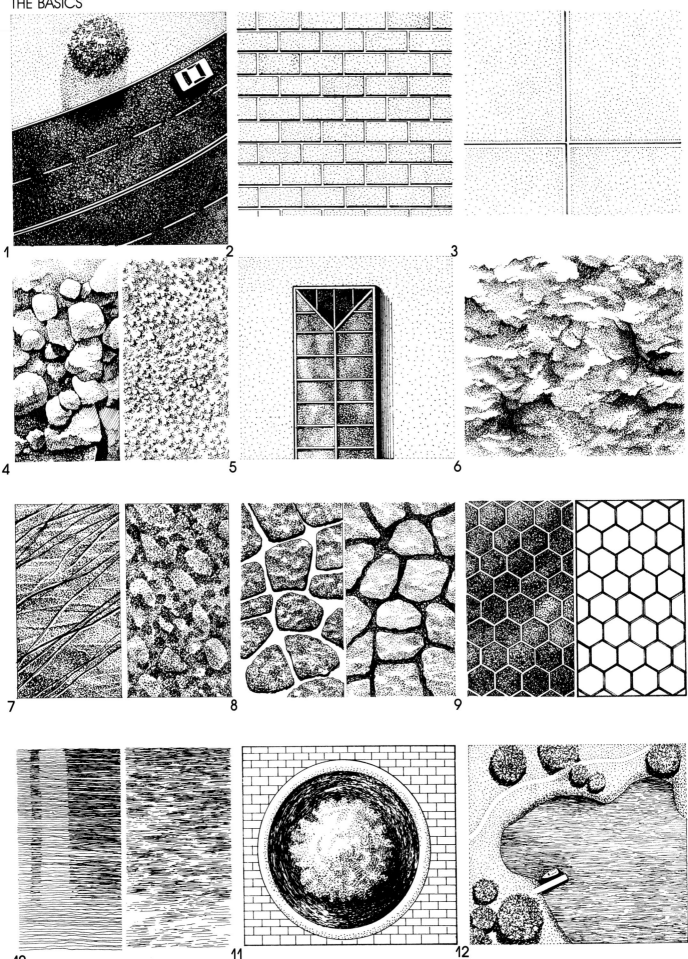

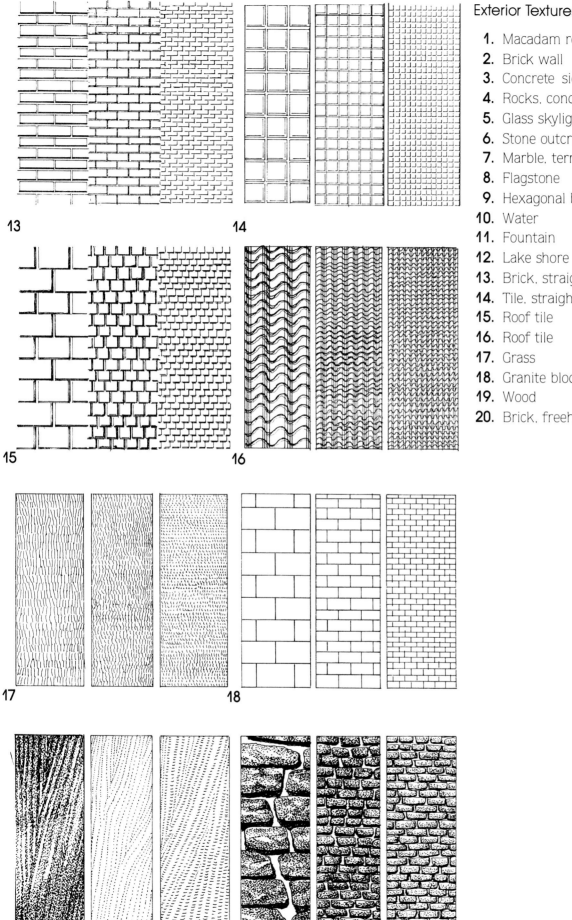

Exterior Textures

1. Macadam road
2. Brick wall
3. Concrete sidewalk
4. Rocks, concrete
5. Glass skylight
6. Stone outcropping
7. Marble, terracotta
8. Flagstone
9. Hexagonal block
10. Water
11. Fountain
12. Lake shore
13. Brick, straightedge
14. Tile, straightedge
15. Roof tile
16. Roof tile
17. Grass
18. Granite block
19. Wood
20. Brick, freehand

13

14

15

16

17

18

19

20

Chapter 2: ENTOURAGE

Entourage is what we call everything that supports a drawing. *Entourage* is a French word meaning "surroundings."

Entourage includes people, cars, trees, furniture, and so on.

Remember that entourage must support your drawing and not dominate it. When drawing people, for instance, make sure that they are in scale with your building or interior. The figures should not intrude. Do not draw a person looking out at the viewer and making a face. The people should be in character with the drawing.

Trees, grass, flowers, bushes, and other landscape details are also important; they soften your drawing. Again, make sure they are in scale.

Cars, trucks, planes, or boats may also be part of your drawing. Be sure that the vehicles are drawn properly on a street, that they are recognizable, and that the scale is correct.

In summary, entourage makes your drawing believable, but to achieve believability, you must make the details accurate and the layout precise. This will come with practice and repetition.

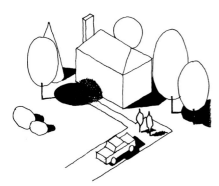

Entourage

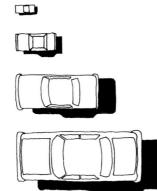

Figures that intrude

Figures that do not intrude

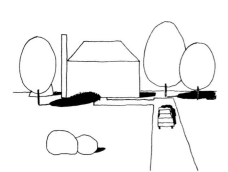

Trees and grass

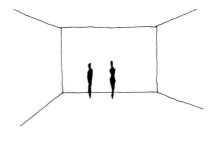

Cars

PEOPLE

Minimum personality but correct scale—these are the two most important characteristics of the people that inhabit drawings. They are in our drawings for only one reason: to give a sense of reality and scale. Do not overdraw the faces. Make sure the fashions and hairstyles are up-to-date.

Tailor the people to the drawing. After determining the correct scale, give them the proper attire. In a business setting, the men and women should be carrying briefcases and look like businesspeople. Airports require luggage; street scenes may need people in coats or jackets. Also show action if it will enhance the atmosphere. Have people walking along streets, talking together, or sitting at desks—in short, doing anything that will logically fill your drawing. Here are some examples to copy or imitate.

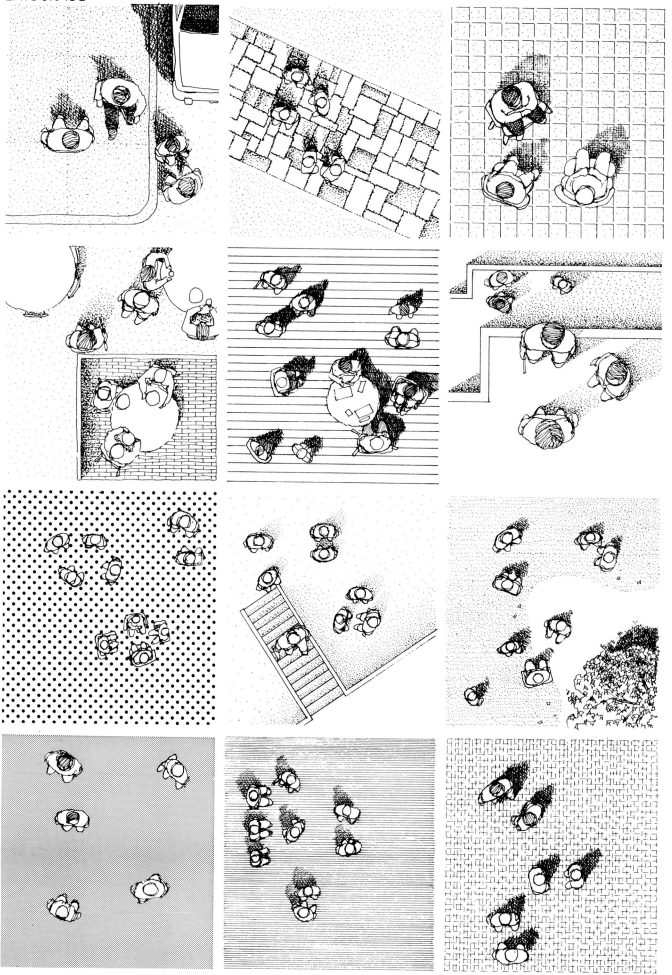

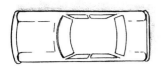

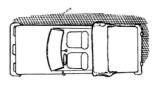

There will be times when you will have to draw in plan (viewing the object from above). These illustrations show examples of people and cars in plan. You can see in these little sketches how light, shadow, and texture are used to describe the setting.

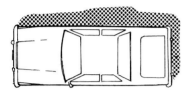

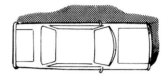

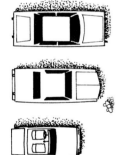

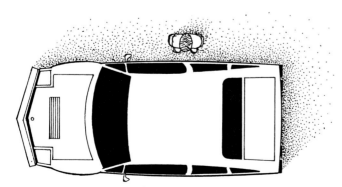

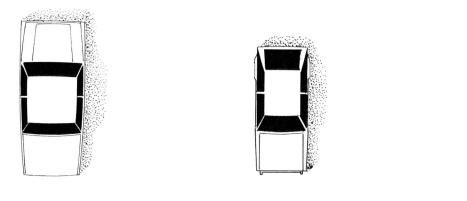

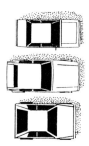

CARS AND TRUCKS IN PLAN

The illustrations show examples of cars in plan. Notice that some depiction of shadows helps to create dimension.

Groups of cars and trucks often must be shown in plan. They can be kept very simple, yet still need to reflect actual scale.

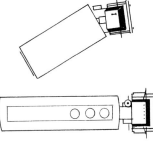

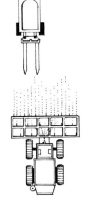

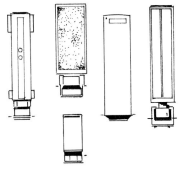
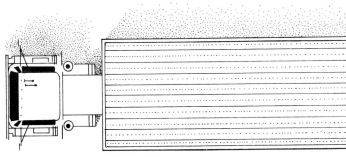

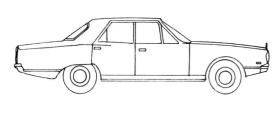

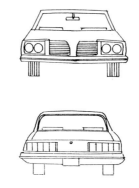

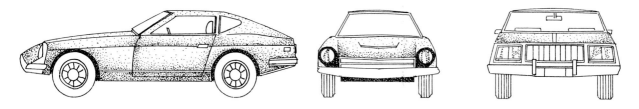

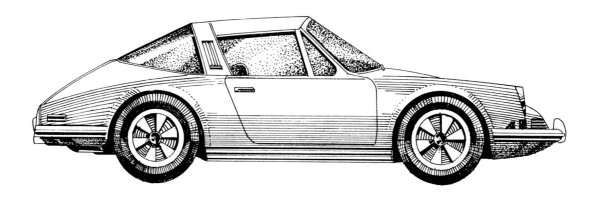

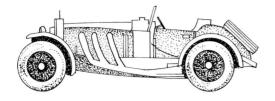

CARS AND TRUCKS IN ELEVATION

Rendering an automobile in elevation leaves room for adding much more detail than in plan drawings. These cars and trucks give you a good range of styles and types to imitate.

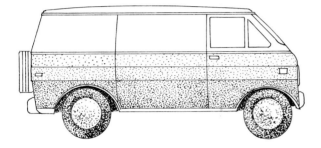

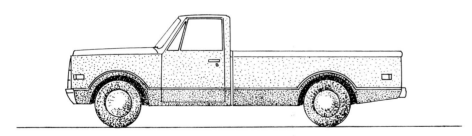

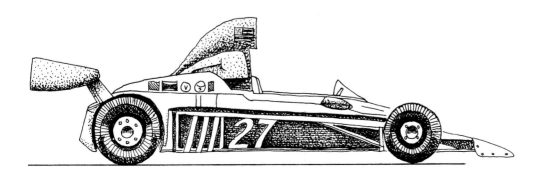

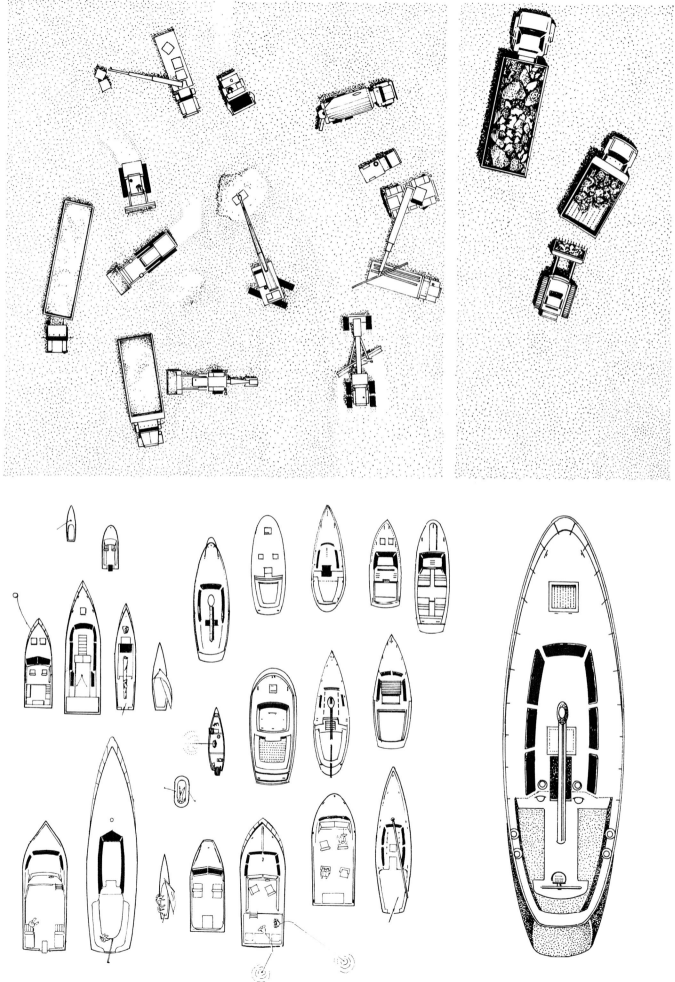

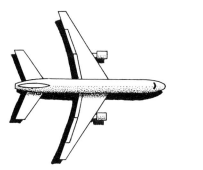
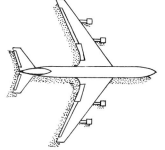

Occasionally drawings also call for construction equipment, boats, or planes to be drawn in plan. These illustrations show some of the variety that can be achieved.

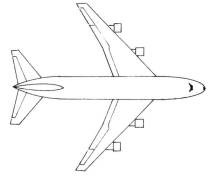

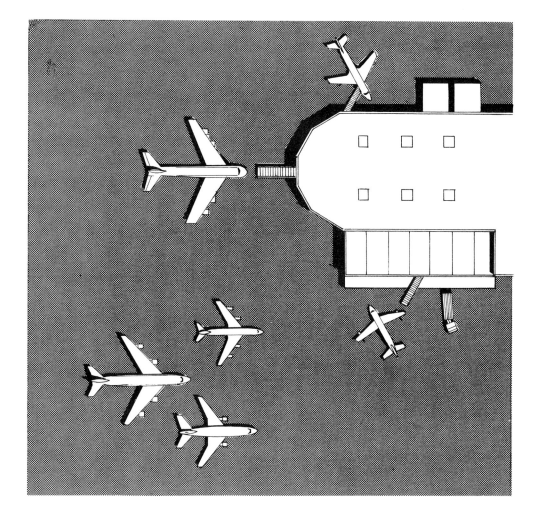

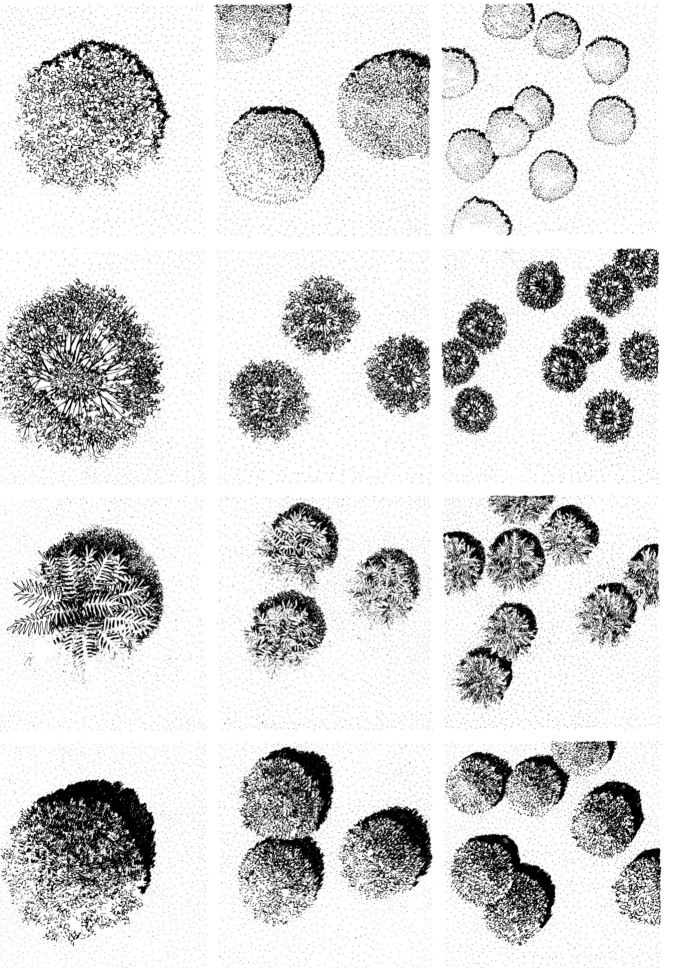

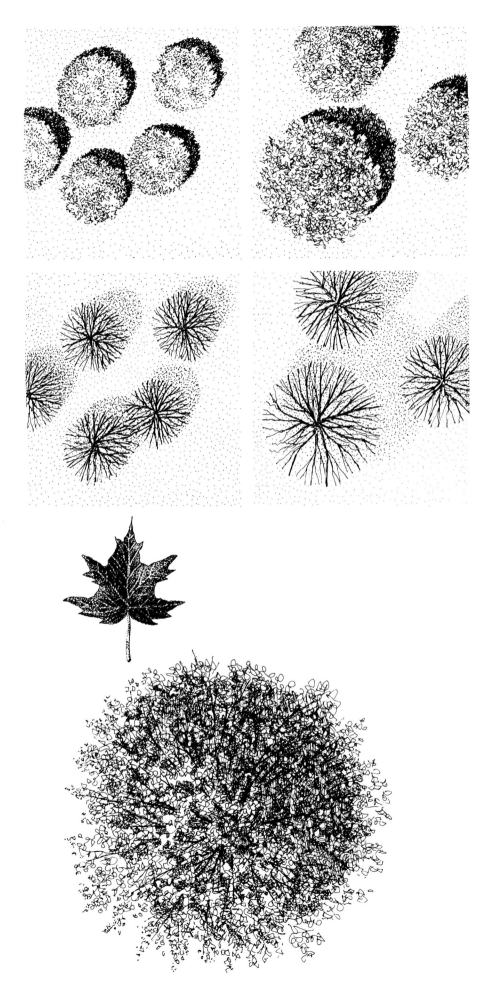

TREES AND BUSHES IN PLAN

Trees and bushes are very important to any exterior drawing. A
beautiful landscape can make the
setting look inviting. Here are
some examples of trees drawn in
plan. Notice the variety in shrub-
bery types that can be achieved
easily.

TREES IN ELEVATION

You will usually want to draw trees and bushes in elevation. Learn to draw single trees as well as trees in groups. Notice how variations in shading can clearly delineate which trees are in the foreground and which are in the back.

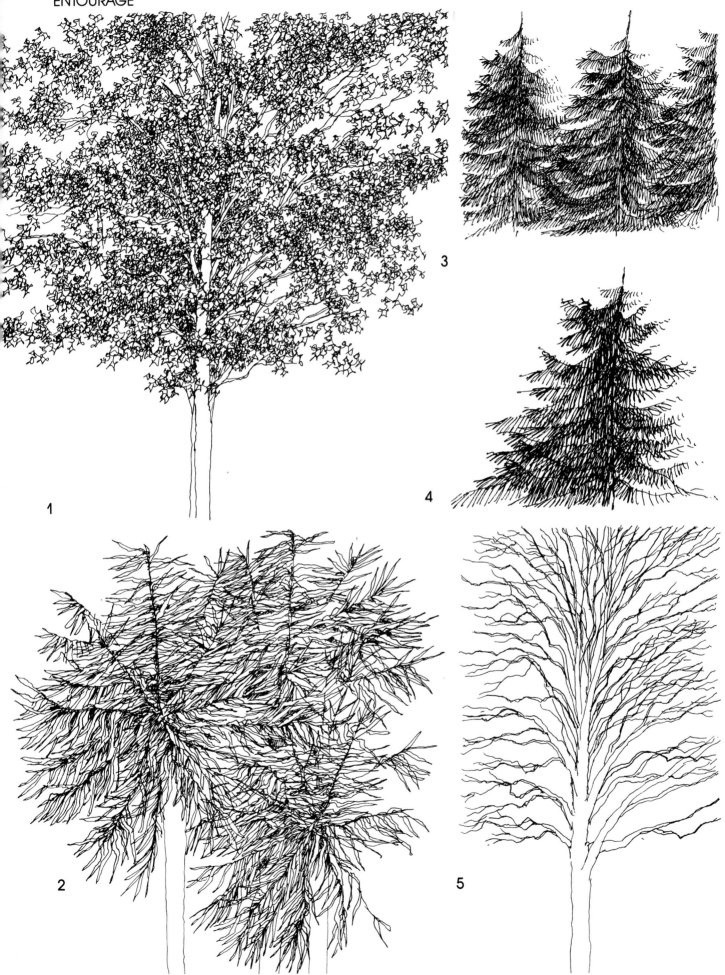

1

2

3

4

5

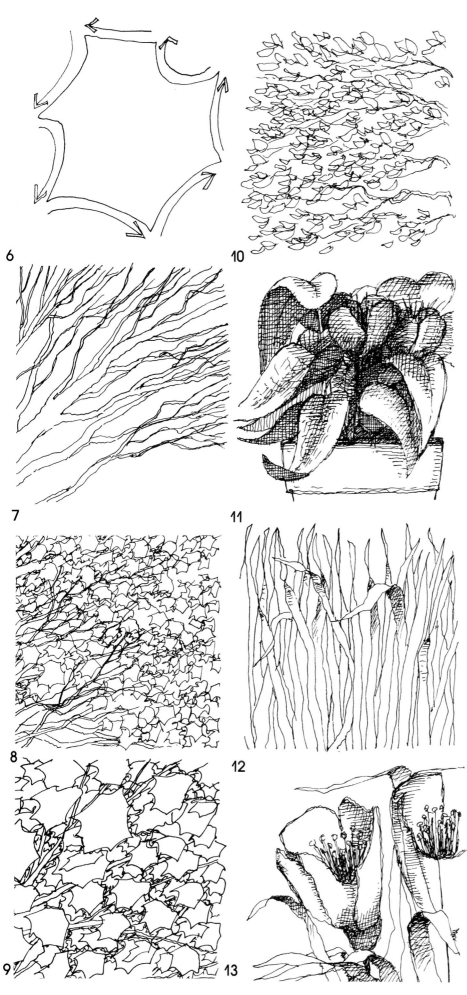

6

10

7

11

8

12

9

13

TREE COMPONENTS

These examples show the finished trees and their components. Yes, you must draw each branch and each leaf individually in order to achieve the types of whole trees shown in illustrations 1 through 5. You must practice drawing the branches and leaves shown in illustrations 7 through 10. Illustration 6 shows the way to draw an individual leaf. Trace this leaf and then draw it over and over in different sizes. Do this until you feel that you can draw leaves easily. Then try to imitate the way leaves group on a tree branch: some small, some large. To draw a complete tree, draw the branch outline first, then fill the branches with leaves of varying sizes. Don't get discouraged—this takes practice.

Illustrations 11 through 13 show examples of other vegetation that can be used as entourage.

Chapter 3: SITE PLAN

The site plan is a two-dimensional representation of a building or buildings, bridge, highway, trees, river, or the like showing only the planes that are parallel to the ground.

You might look at it another way. Imagine you are in a helicopter looking straight down, so you can see only the tops of objects and buildings—no sides, just tops.

A site plan is extremely important in any graphic presentation because it shows the location of a structure while allowing the viewer to understand the relation-ship of the structure to the ground. The site plan is also important because it shows the relationship of a building to its surroundings.

In order to draw a site plan, you must understand not only the textures that make up the building but those that surround it as well. Therefore, before attempting a site plan, you need to have mastered the skills presented in Chapter 2.

You must know how to draw trees, earth, grass, and water as well as concrete, steel, brick, and glass. You must know the scale of your drawing and relate it to the materials you are going to draw. This takes imagination and research.

The source of the light is an important variable when you are drawing a site plan, since it allows the viewer to realize the heights of the various objects in the plan. The shadow of a thirty-foot tree, for instance, is longer than that of a car, assuming they are both drawn under the same conditions (that is, the source of light is the same for both).

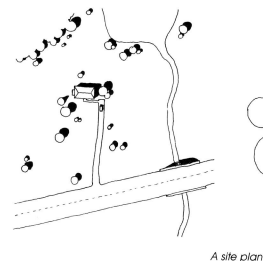

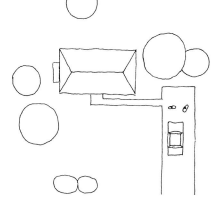

A site plan

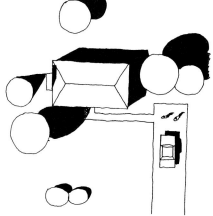

The light source

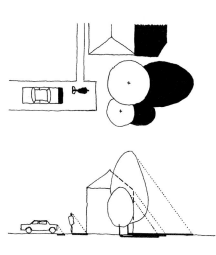

Trees and grass

Light direction

1

2

3

4

5

6

7

8

9

10

11

12

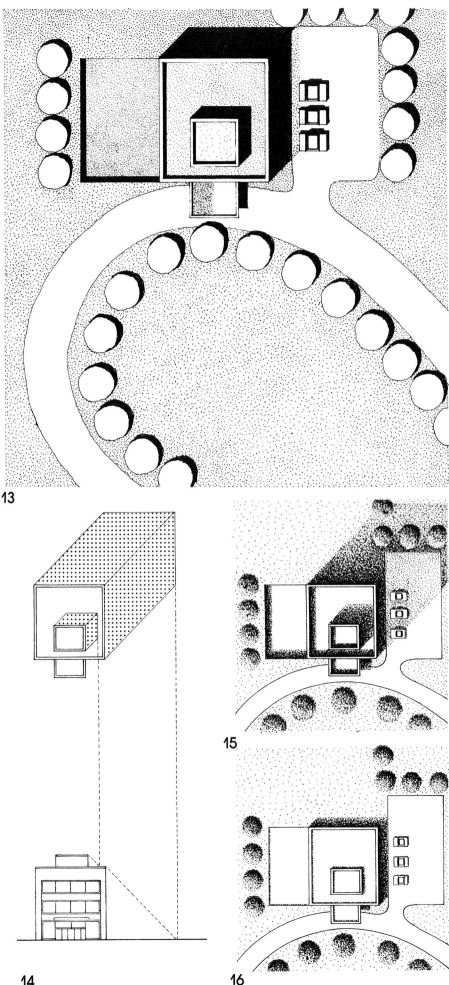

13

14

15

16

DRAWING THE SITE PLAN

The best way to understand how to draw a site plan is to draw one, so here in simple steps is how it is done.

1. Imagine you are looking directly down at a building; no perspective at all is involved. You can see only the edges and the top of the roof. You cannot see the faces (sides) of the building.

2. Draw just what you see, in any scale. This is a site plan. To make it more exciting, you will need to add shadow and texture.

3. Adding shadows will make your drawing read as a building. Adding shadows to the ground gives the building height and dimension.

4. A small-scale site plan shows shadows and trees.

5. A large-scale site plan shows more of the building, less of the surroundings.

6. A middle-scale site plan shows an appropriate amount of building and surroundings.

7. Stipple technique. Note how evenly the dots are placed, how the shadow is darker as it gets closer to the building.

8. Line technique. All shadows were done with line work.

9. Solid ink shadow. A very quick technique: all shadows are done as solids.

10–12. These drawings show pencil shadow, line drawing without shadow, and soft pencil shadow.

13. Note the textures, details, and technique of this illustration.

14. Here is a simple diagram of shadow construction.

15 and **16.** The character of a drawing can be changed by varying the length of the shadow.

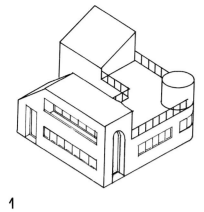

1

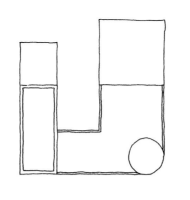

2

3

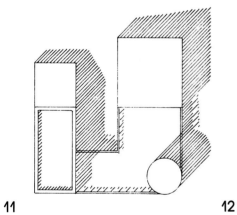

6

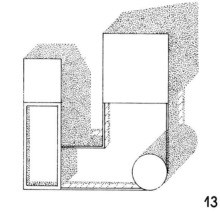

7

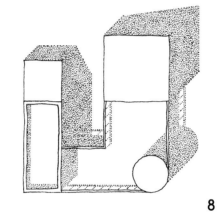

8

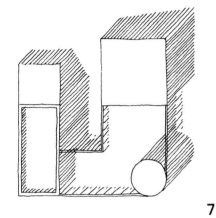

11

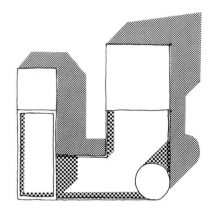

12

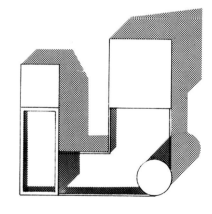

13

16

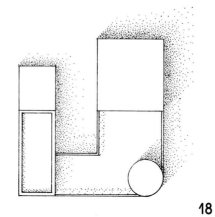

17

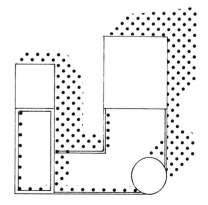

18

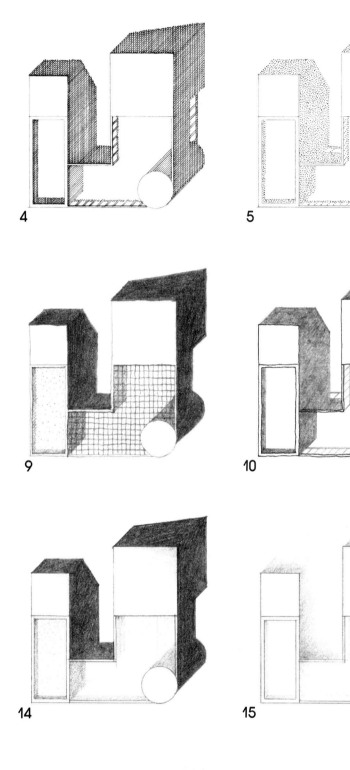

4

5

9

10

14

15

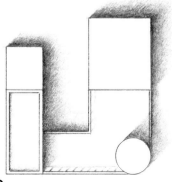

19

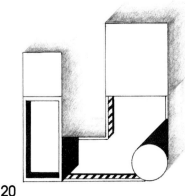

20

STYLES

Any drawing that you delineate may be drawn with a variety of techniques and with a variety of materials. Shown here are site plans of the same building using different techniques: freehand and straightedge, pencil and pen. The idea is that not only are there many ways to delineate the same building, but the possible combinations are infinite.

1. The building

2. A simple freehand drawing

3. Straightedge drawing with solid ink shadow

4. Straightedge with line shadow

5. Straightedge with light stipple or dotted shadow

6. Freehand drawing with single line shadow

7. Freehand with heavy stipple shadow

8. Freehand with two different types of Zipatone for shadow

9. Freehand with a combination of line, stipple, and solid ink shadow

10. Freehand with solid ink shadow

11. Straightedge with straightedge shadow

12. Straightedge with stippling

13. Straightedge with solid ink and Zipatone

14. Freehand with solid ink shadow, pencil, and light stippling

15. Straightedge with pencil shadow

16. Straightedge with line and stippling shadow

17. Straightedge with stippling that fades

18. Straightedge with Zipatone texture for shadow

19. Straightedge with pencil shadow

20. Straightedge with combination pencil, solid ink shadow

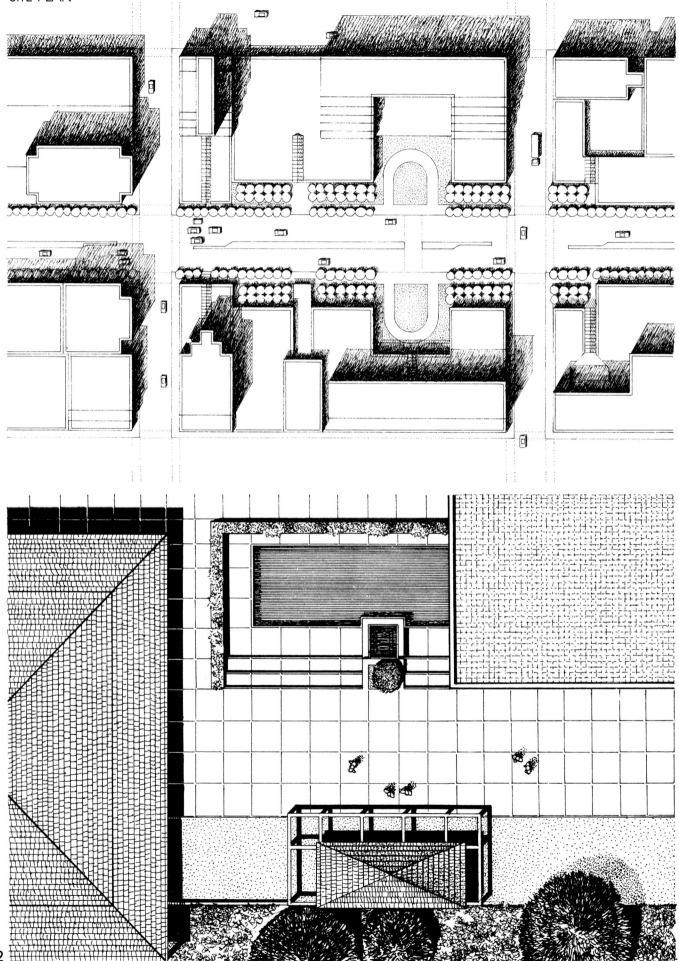

1

2

VARIOUS SITE PLANS

These four site plans have been delineated at various scales and in different styles. Be aware of the combination of textures and the technique of completion.

1. Large-scale site plan. The trees are circles. The shadow is a freehand line. The drawing itself is done using a straightedge.

2. Smaller-scale drawing. A courtyard and fountain. Notice the tile textures, the people, and the trees.

3. This plan used a combination of pencil and pen textures.

4. A beach house. Notice the texture of the water and the sand.

3

4

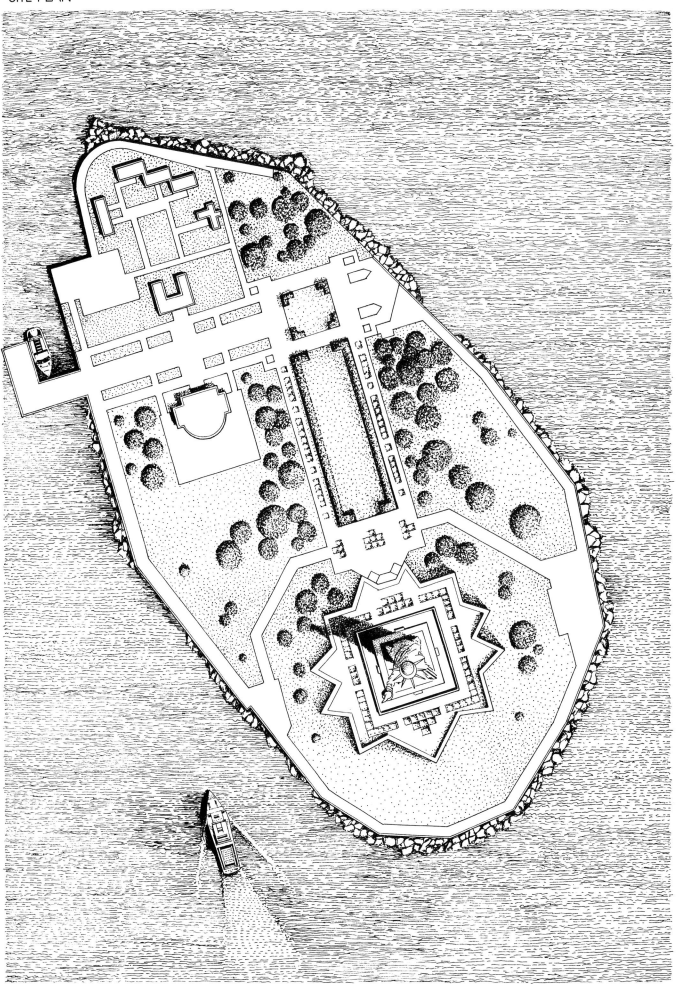

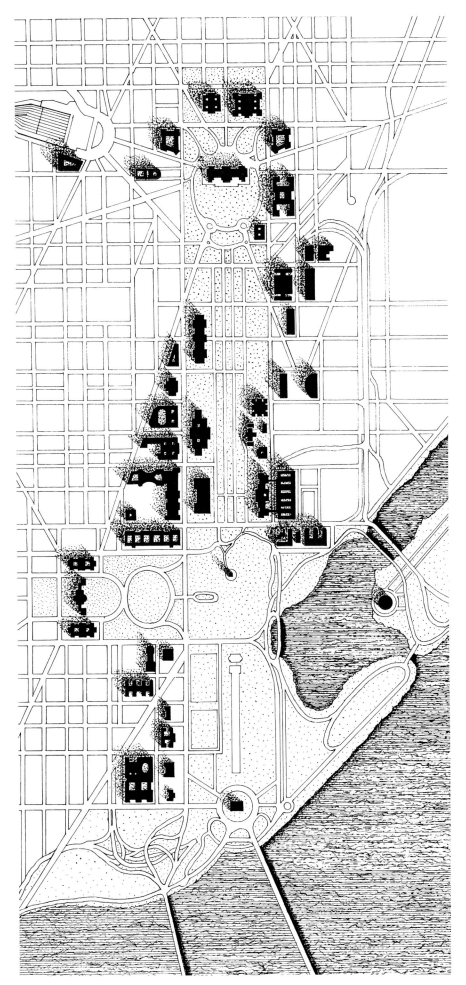

LIBERTY ISLAND

Site plan drawn in pen and ink. This drawing was done using a straightedge. The quality of a straightedge drawing is totally different from that of a freehand drawing. Notice the texture of the water and how it is delineated. Grass and trees are drawn by stippling (dots). Make sure that the textures work together and that the scale of your drawing remains consistent.

WASHINGTON, D.C.

A site plan done in a more stylized manner. This is a simple method for showing a large-scale area.

Chapter 4: FLOOR PLAN

In a plan view, whether a site plan or a floor plan, the view is from above looking directly down. Imagine a room, then imagine a gigantic knife cutting through the walls of the room, about five feet from the floor. When you look directly down, what you see is called a floor plan. You see the entire contents of the room from above. Everything you see, you see in plan view—that is, you see the top of everything.

When drawing a plan view, you must decide how to delineate all the objects that will be in your drawing. There are no hard-and-fast rules about how to delineate objects in plan. You must imagine what something might look like when you are looking directly down at it, and work from there. Besides using your imagination to visualize, you will find it also helps to look at as many plan drawings as possible. Other designers' drawings can give you some insight into how to delineate a plan view.

The problem you face with a plan view is the flat appearance of all the objects in the space. This problem is overcome by the introduction of light. Light produces shadow; taller objects have longer shadows, smaller objects smaller shadows. The shadows, therefore, allow the viewer to judge the distance each object is above the ground.

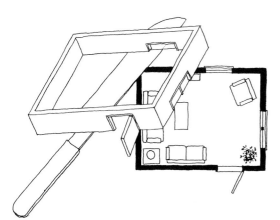

The floor plan

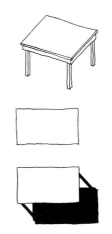

Flattening objects

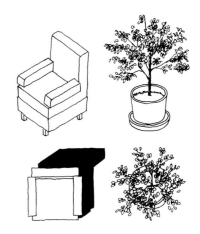

Adding shadow

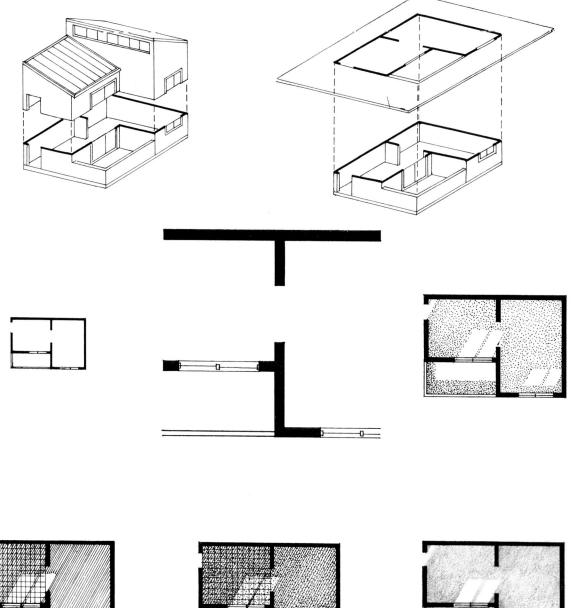
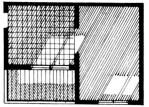
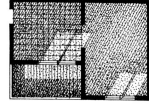
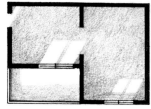
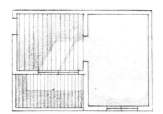
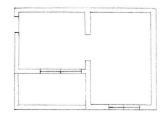
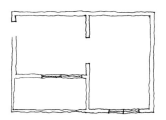

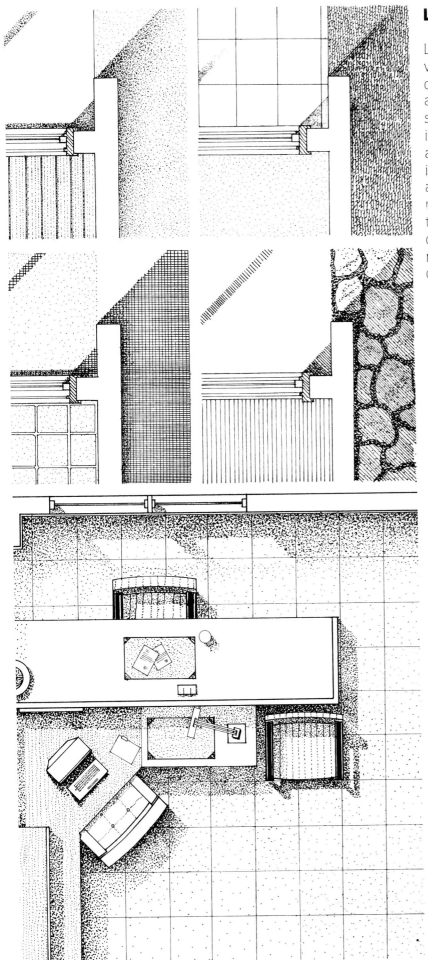

LIGHT AND TEXTURE

Light and texture are the two variables that you must control in order to delineate an understandable floor plan. The following series of drawings was done using various techniques, scales, and textures. They give a general idea of how to go about drawing a floor plan. Notice how pen and pencil have been combined. As the scale of a plan drawing increases, the delineation of materials must be done more carefully and with greater detail.

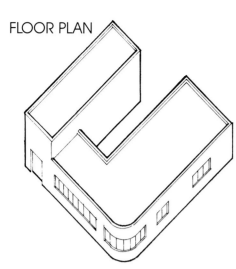

FLOOR PLAN

1

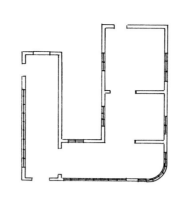

2

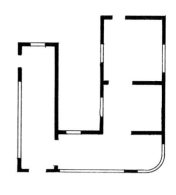

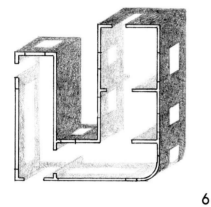

5

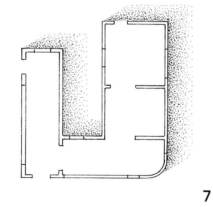

6

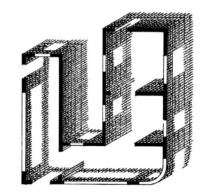

7

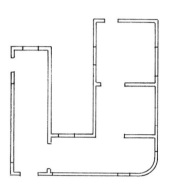

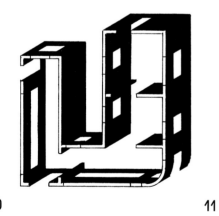

10

11

12

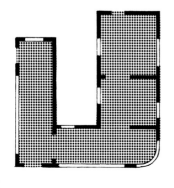

15

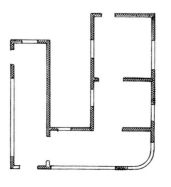

16

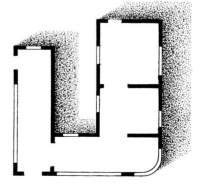

17

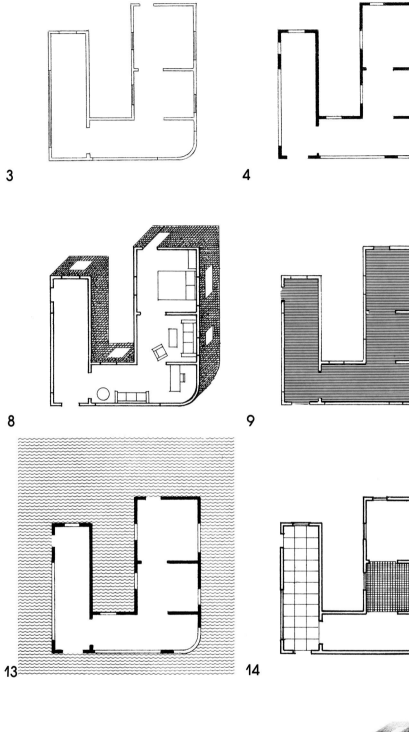

3

4

8

9

13

14

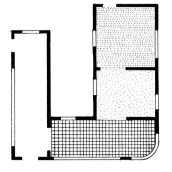

18

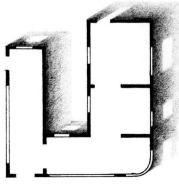

19

FLOOR PLAN POSSIBILITIES

These drawings will give you an idea of the endless variety of presentations possible for even the simplest of floor plans. Each one was drawn with a straight-edge, pen, and ink, but as you can see, each takes on a different feeling depending on the textures and shadows used.

1. Ink outline indicating walls and windows
2. Solid ink walls; blank windows
3. Pencil outline
4. Solid pencil line for walls
5. Pencil shadow
6. Stipple shadow
7. Single line
8. Straightedge crosshatched shadow
9. Solid-line floor space
10. Solid ink shadow
11. Straightedge line shadow
12. Freehand line shadow
13. Zipatone texture surrounding with solid ink walls
14. Floor tile textures
15. Zipatone texture floors
16. Zipatone texture walls only
17. Stipple shadow that fades out; solid ink walls
18. Solid ink walls with varying floor textures
19. Solid ink walls with pencil shadow

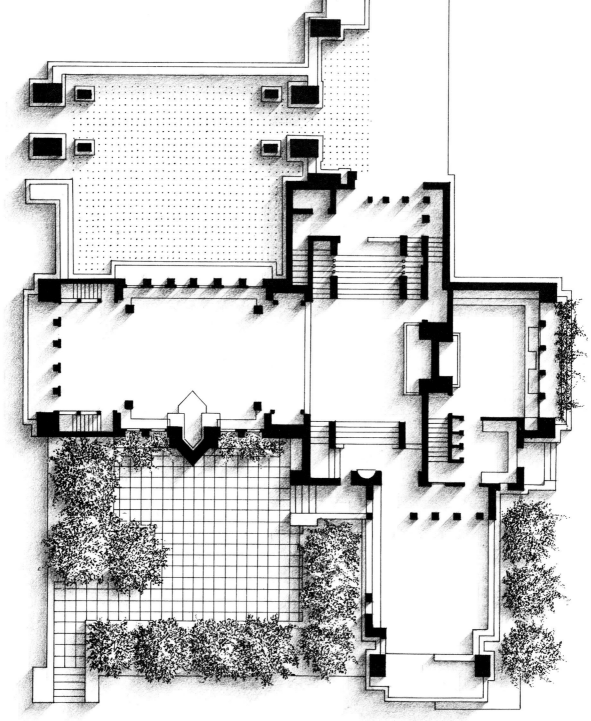

1

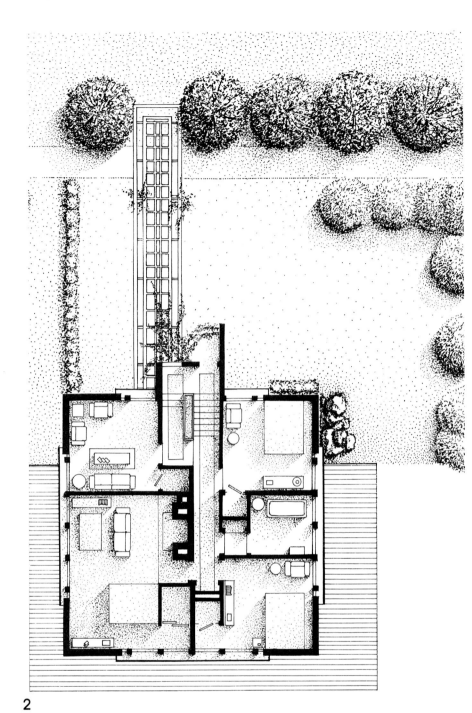

2

STRAIGHTEDGE PLANS

Shown here is a series of pen-and-ink floor plans done using a straightedge. Note the textures and the delineation of the furniture. The addition of furniture gives the viewer an understanding of the use of each space.

1. In this drawing, the trees surrounding the building are extremely important. Care was given to delineate the planting and trees to depict a beautiful outdoor space. The floor textures are different types of tile, done with a combination of stippling and line work.

2. Stippling, or dots, is the major ingredient of this floor plan. The interior textures, the shadows, the trees, bushes, and grass—all are produced with varying densities of stippling.

3. With a small-scale floor plan, it is more professional to simplify interior texture and line work. The exterior texture, which in this case is stippling, sets off the interior.

4. This is another small-scale floor plan, but here cast shadows from the walls give a feeling of depth.

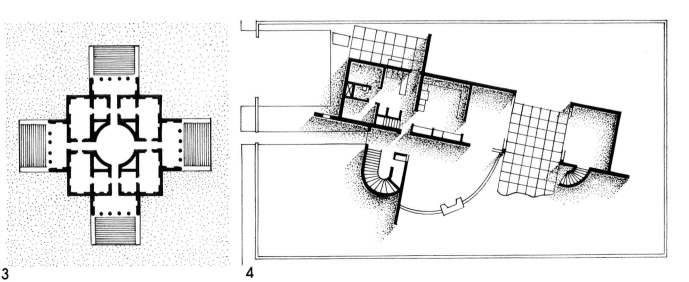

3   4

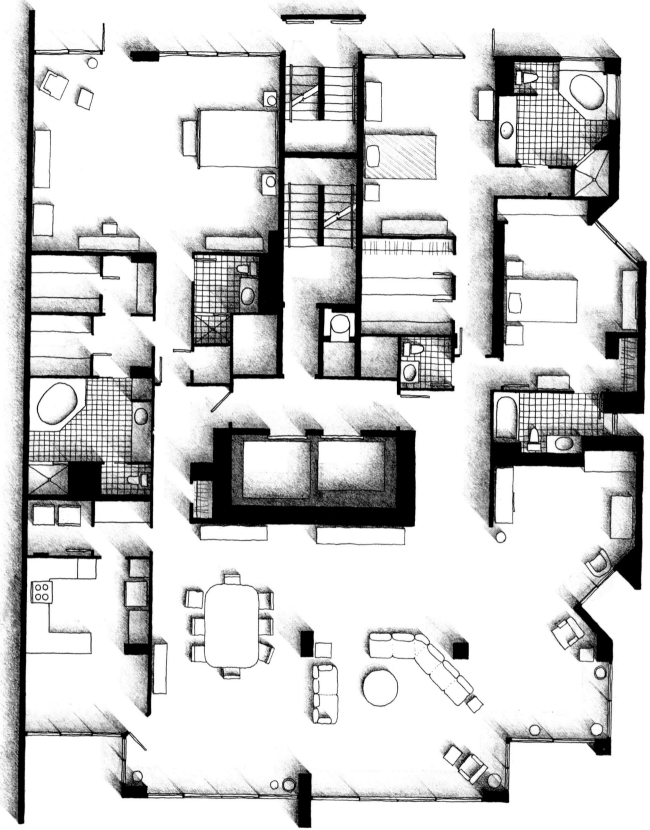

1

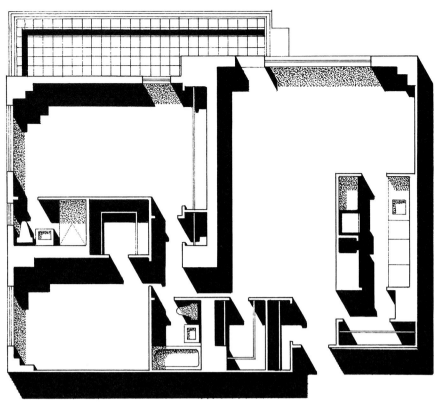

2

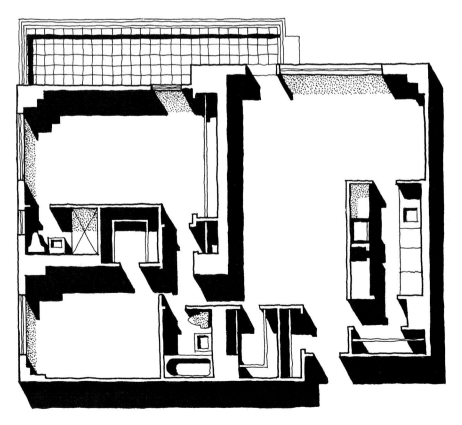

3

TEXTURED FLOOR PLANS

The carefully delineated floor plan is an extremely important part of any architectural presentation. It is a balance of the architecture and all the supporting elements.

1. This is a carefully drawn plan, actually done freehand (freehand means a freehand pen line drawn over a straightedge pencil line). As you begin to draw freehand, always work over a straightedge line. It will give you more control.

Light is what makes this drawing work. Without a light source, the drawing would have no visual interest. Notice that the shadows are rendered in pencil so that they don't visually overpower the walls.

2. This drawing is a straightedge floor plan with the walls left white. The three-dimensional effect is achieved with a solid black shadow. Notice the stipple shadow that is thrown by the glass.

3. This drawing is the same as the previous plan but was done freehand. Notice the difference in character.

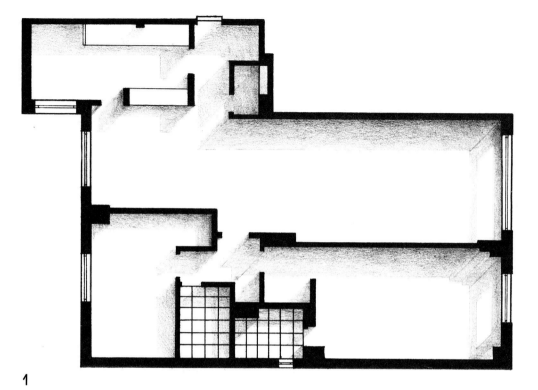

1

3

ADDING PERSPECTIVE

It can sometimes create interest if a floor plan is drawn with perspective rather than as a bird's-eye view.

1. This is simple, straightforward floor plan—no furniture, minimal shadow.

2. A bit more complexity has been added to this floor plan. Furniture and texture add to the visual interest of the drawing.

3. A vanishing point has been added and the plans of this multistory building have been stacked on top of one another.

4. By locating the vanishing point at a greater distance from the floor plan, the feeling and look of the plan are changed.

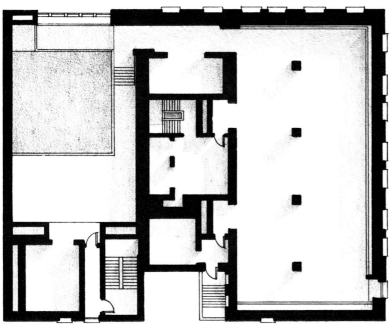

2

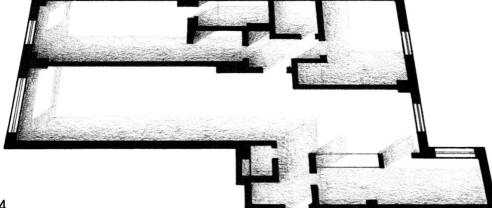

4

Chapter 5: **ELEVATION**

An elevation is a technical drawing that delineates the outer skin of a building. It is a drawing that is used in the construction of a building. Because this type of drawing is so simple to construct, it has become a presentation tool for the designer. It is a simple drawing because no perspective is involved.

When drawing an elevation, it is extremely important to delineate the hierarchy of the planar surfaces, or what is in front of what. Through strength of line and texture, you make the viewer understand the surface of your building or the surface of your interior.

Line Quality

The line, and how it is drawn, is all-important. Whether to use a straightedge or work freehand is the first important decision. You make this decision based on the character that you want your drawing to have. The freehand drawing will have a looser, less technical quality than the precise, straightedge drawing.

Examine the freehand line

compared to the straightedge line. What are the characteristics of each? The sketch quality of the freehand line lends itself to stone and brick, irregular materials. If you try to delineate a brick wall with a straightedge, you will find that the character of your drawing will be false. A brick is not exact; it does not have a precise edge. Brick should be drawn freehand to give it the irregular quality that it needs.

A contemporary building of glass and steel, on the other hand, should be drawn with a straightedge, since the drawing will reflect the architectural precision of the building.

Light Source

Next, the source of light must be decided. Light gives the viewer a better understanding of the planes and surfaces of the building. Once you have established the light source and the hierarchy of line and plane, you must choose the materials of the project—brick, concrete, glass, and so on—and decide how to delineate them.

Surface Texture

The surface of the building is very important in any elevation drawing. The textures are what make the drawing "read." The textures do not necessarily have to be uniform; they can vary. There may be highlights within the elevation. Try, as much as possible, to mix your textures so that you create highlights and dark and light areas. No matter what you are drawing, whether it is simple or complex, there must be a variance in textures in light and shadow.

Change the intensity of the textures; mix them. Develop darker areas by overlapping lines, not by painting in black. The subtlety of pencil allows you to realize textures that you cannot achieve with pen and ink. You can shade from dark to light more simply with pencil. In addition, a pencil drawing can be done in much less time than one in pen and ink, so at certain times it is a necessary way to draw.

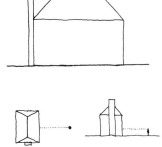

The elevation

The light source

Adding surface texture

ELEVATION

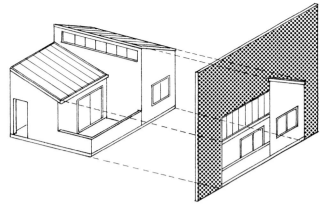

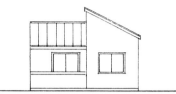

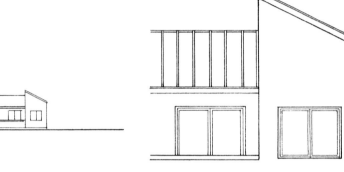

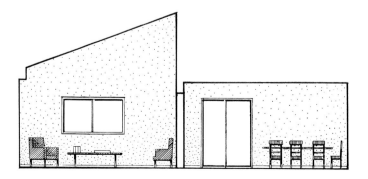

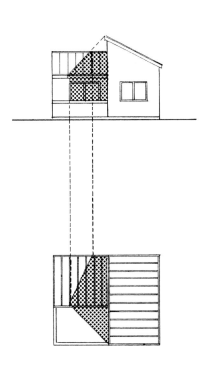

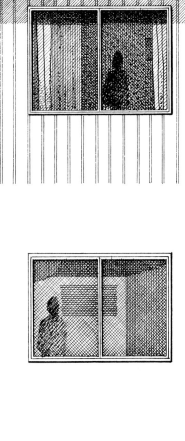

ELEVATION COMPONENTS

Here you can see exactly how an elevation is drawn. The drawings show the components of an elevation and where each comes from in the anatomy of the architecture. Compare the pencil and pen techniques and notice how each defines the construction of shadows, the treatment of glass, and the delineation of building materials. By mixing these techniques, and by practicing the textures, you will start to evolve your own style.

Glass

Glass can be delineated in several ways. It may be transparent: we look through the glass and see the interior. This usually works for interior projects and small-scale drawings. When delineating the transparency of glass, remember your light source, textures, and materials.

Alternatively, glass may be reflective: there is a strong light source that eliminates the ability to see into the building. The glass reflects what is in front of the building. When you draw glass that is reflective, it is important not to let the drawing become too busy. It is better to simplify the reflection than to let it become complicated and photographic. Especially if the surface of the building you are delineating is full of details, it is a good idea to let the treatment of the glass remain simple.

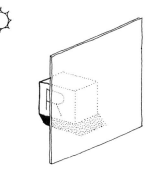

Drawing glass

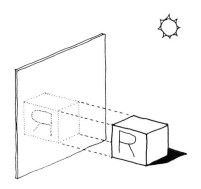

Reflection

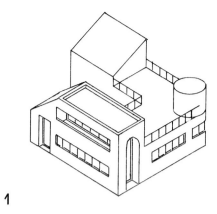

1

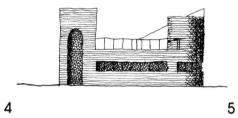

2

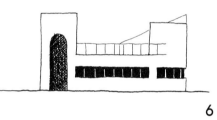

3

4

5

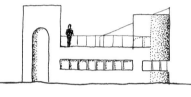

6

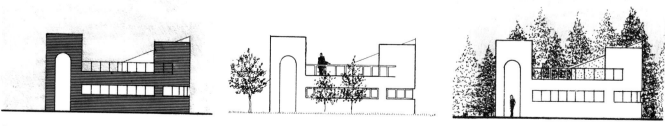

7

8

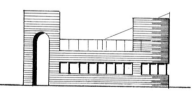

9

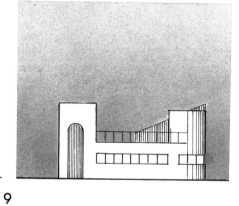

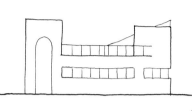

10

11

12

ADDING CHARACTER

The character of an elevation changes with the line, textures, and entourage. Throughout this group of drawings the building remains the same, but the background, foreground, shadows, and glass treatment change, altering the character of the entire drawing. Basically, the changes are made by mixing and matching techniques.

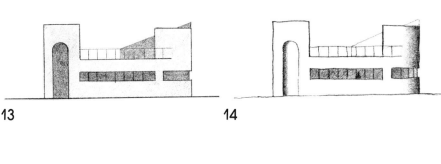

13   14

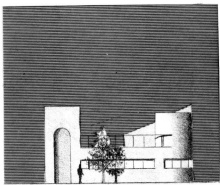

15   16

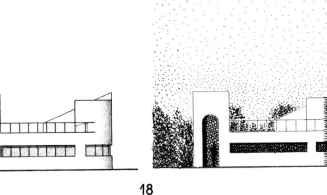

17   18

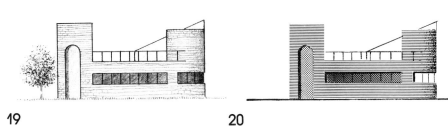

19   20

1. Small perspective drawing
2. Freehand ink drawing
3. Straightedge ink drawing, spray background
4. Freehand ink drawing, freehand brick texture
5. Freehand ink drawing, solid glass, no texture
6. Freehand ink drawing, stipple texture
7. Straightedge ink drawing, stipple texture in sky
8. Straightedge ink drawing, horizontal straight-line texture
9. Straightedge ink drawing, vertical texture, spray background
10. Straightedge ink drawing, Zipatone texture
11. Straightedge ink drawing, trees in foreground
12. Straightedge ink drawing, trees in background
13. Pencil drawing, abstract texture
14. Freehand drawing, pencil texture
15. Straightedge pencil drawing, Zipatone background
16. Freehand pencil drawing, pencil background
17. Straightedge ink drawing, pencil texture
18. Straightedge ink drawing, straightedge textures
19. Pencil and pen mixture
20. Straightedge ink drawing and Zipatone

FREEHAND ELEVATIONS

These freehand elevations show the relaxed technique mentioned previously. Study and imitate the textures used in completing these drawings.

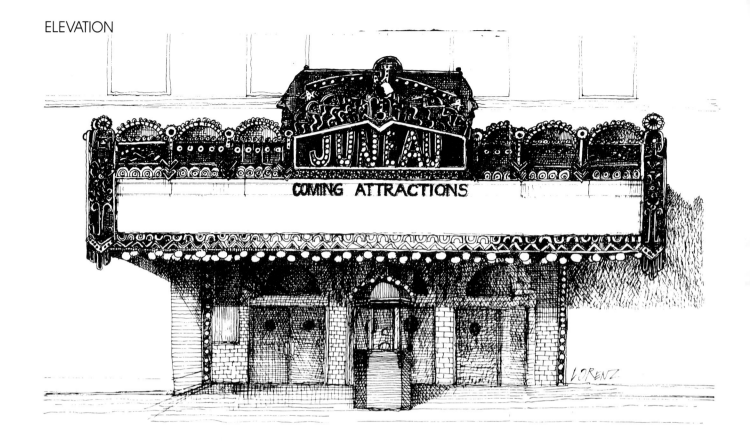

COMING ATTRACTIONS

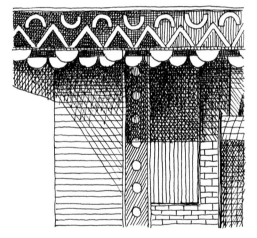

COMBINING METHODS

In these drawings there is a juxtaposition of straightedge and freehand lines. Once again the drawings have been blown up in order that the techniques used would become more evident.

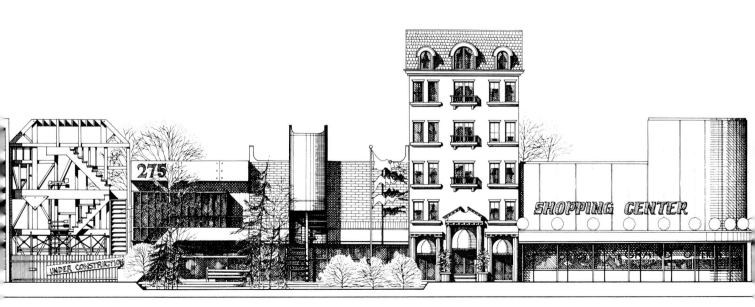

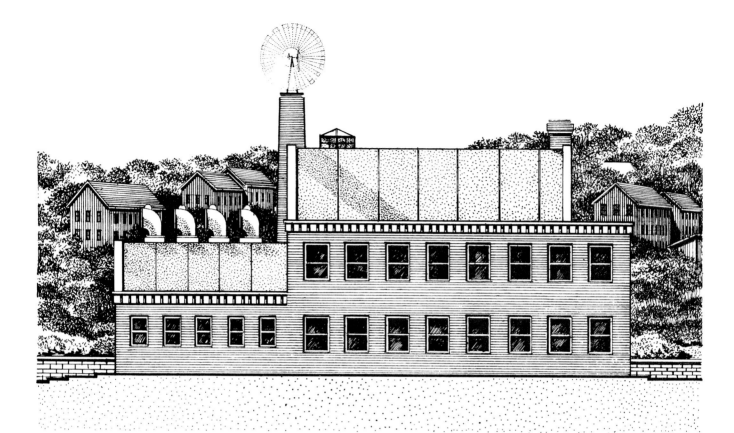

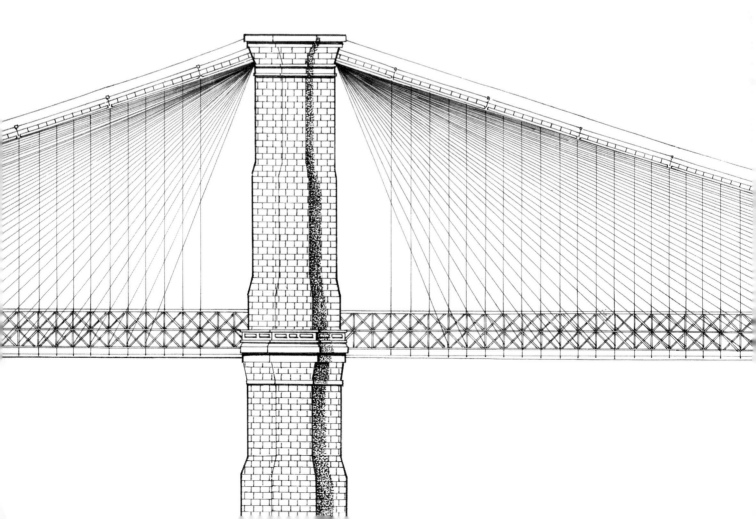

TEXTURE

In these straightedge elevations, notice the mixture of stippling and line. Also be aware of the method of overlaying a finer and heavier pen line to produce the textures that make these drawings "read."

FINE LINE TEXTURE

The dramatic texture and shadow in this next drawing were achieved by using a very fine (no. 0000) pen and working freehand, one line overlaying another. This overlay produces the textures that make the surfaces "read." The facade is not treated as a flat, uninteresting plane; rather, highlights are allowed to happen.

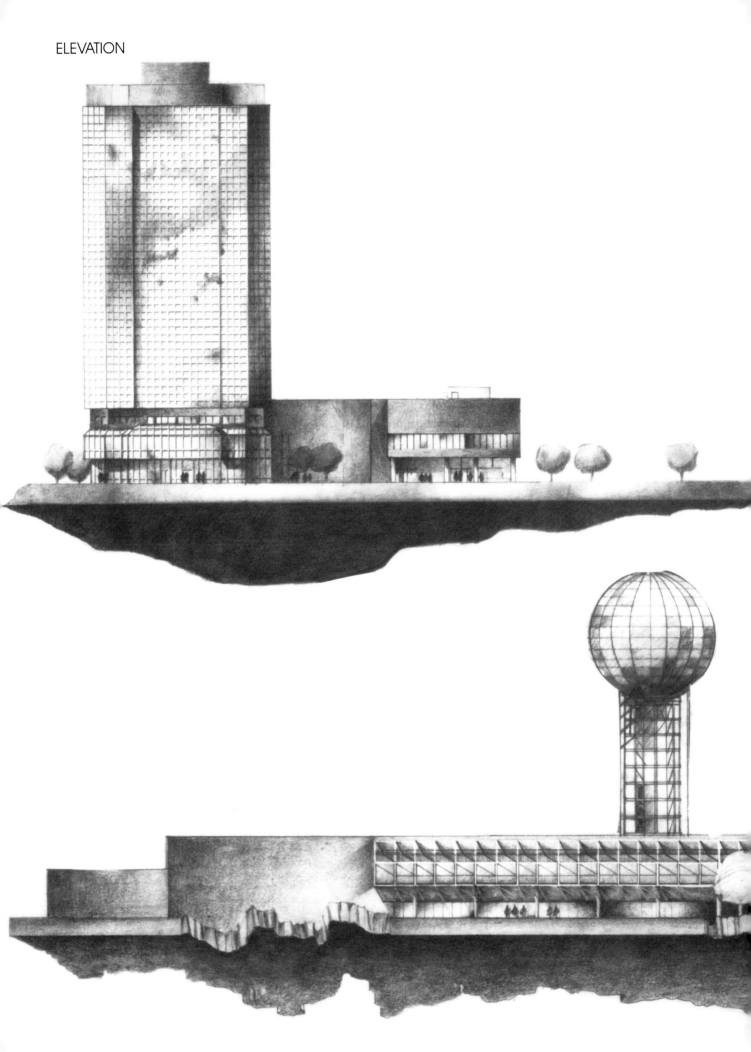

ELEVATION

PENCIL ELEVATIONS

Here are three elevations done entirely in pencil. The difference in character is apparent, as the drawing is much softer than an ink drawing.

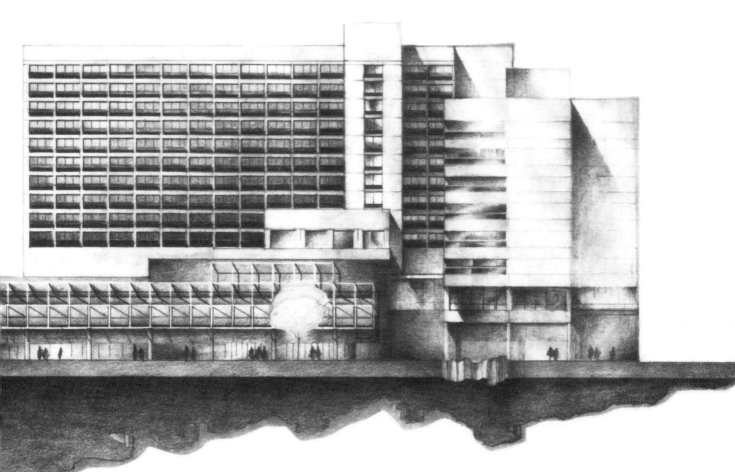

RESTORATIONS

Here are a series of drawings used in restoration projects. Again, notice the techniques used in producing the facades. Remember to work over a straight-edge pencil line to produce all line work and to draw all texture in pencil first before drawing the final ink texture.

Chapter 6: SECTION

Imagine cutting a building vertically from roof to floor with a giant knife. This cut allows you to see the thickness of the ceiling, walls, and floor. If you draw exactly what you see, this drawing is called a section.

A section is a basic architectural drawing done in order to understand the structure, architectural materials, and changes in the level of any building interior. Usually the section does not clarify the depth of the space, and the result is a drawing with a flat quality. It is the job of the illustrator to alter this characteristic, whether the drawing is done in pen and ink, in pencil, or in a combination of both.

Establishing Planes

There is a definite method for eliminating the lack of interest caused by this flat quality. First, establish a hierarchy of planes. Decide which planes within the drawing are advancing and which planes are receding.

The Light Source

Once this decision is made, it allows you to make another decision: the choice of light source. This choice is all-important, since light will cast shadow and create the drama needed within the drawing.

Drawing Technique

After you establish the planes of the section and choose the light source for creating shadow, you need to decide on a drawing technique. This should be based on whether you need a loose freehand treatment, a tight straightedge, or a combination of both. The section cut may be drawn and filled in, or it may be left white. The choice is based on what character you want your drawing to have.

Decide whether black walls will overpower the drawing. Usually this decision will be based on the scale of the drawing. Ink reproduces better than pencil but

does not have pencil's subtlety. Pencil allows you to imitate the effects of light fairly easily. Blending is more easily accomplished with pencil than with pen and ink.

Adding Entourage

The people that inhabit most architectural drawings are important because they permit the viewer to understand the scale of the drawing. Plants and other objects are also an integral part of the drawing. This is especially true for a section drawing.

It is important to develop a quick, distinctive technique for drawing the supporting elements of any drawing. Details are *vital* to drawings and they are *essential* to the professional. Furniture, lighting, and textures give scale and interest. They allow a viewer to wander visually through a drawing and to get involved.

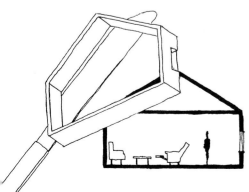

The section

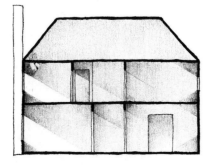

Filled-in section cut

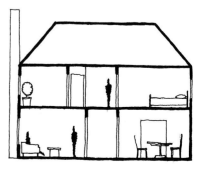

Adding people and furniture

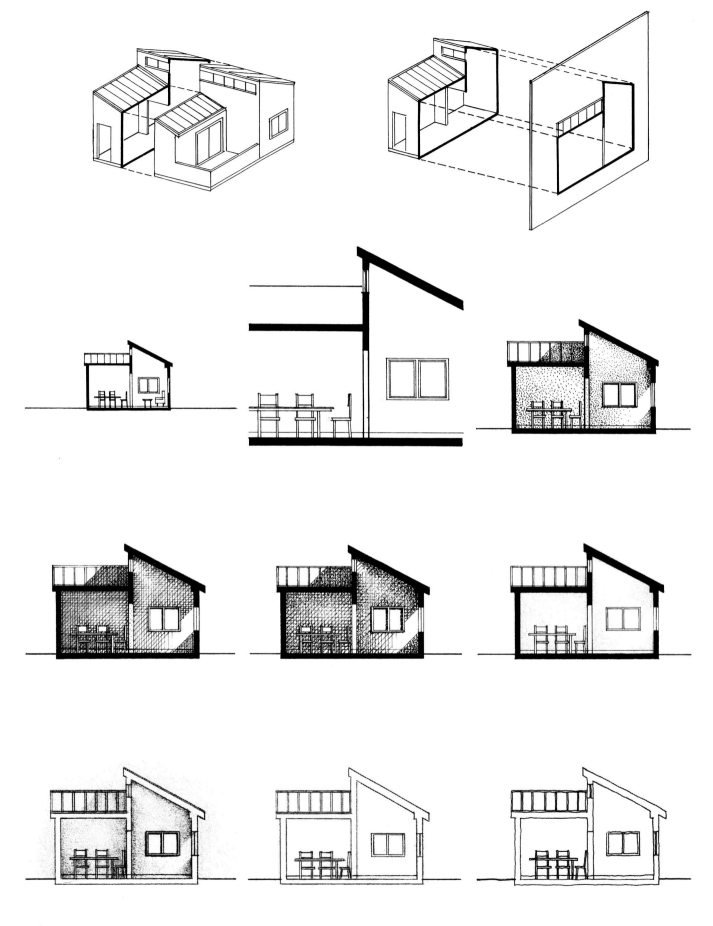

SECTION DRAWINGS

This is a series of drawings done using various techniques, scales, and textures. They give a general idea of how to go about drawing the section. Again, you can see a combination of pencil and pen used to produce a high-contrast section drawing. Notice that as the scale of the drawing increases, the more the materials that are cut through must be shown.

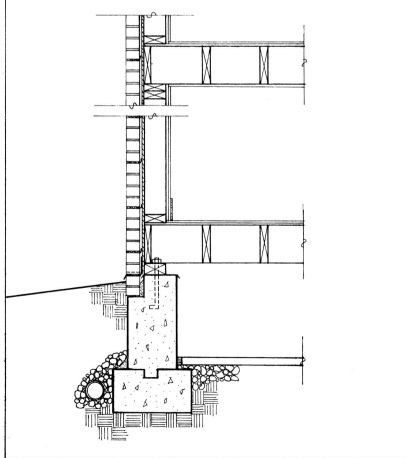

SECTION

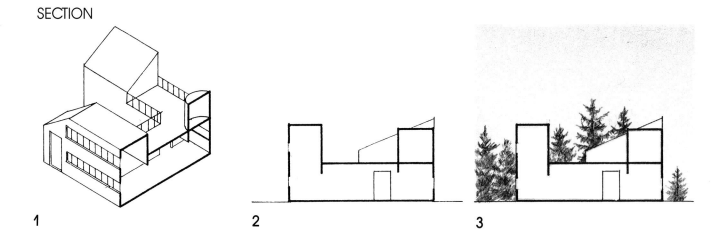

1

2

3

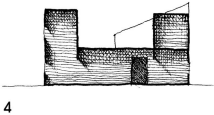

4

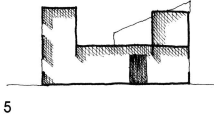

5

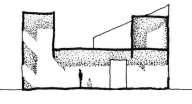

6

7

8

9

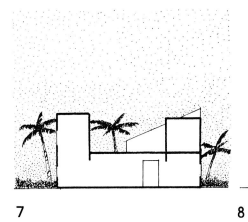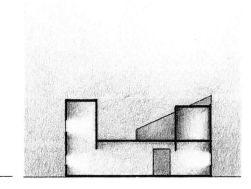

10

11

12

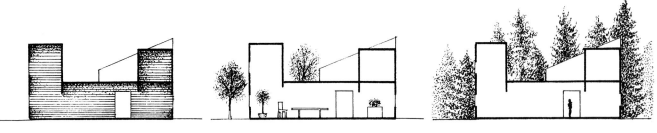

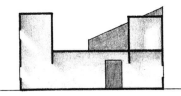

13

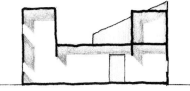

14

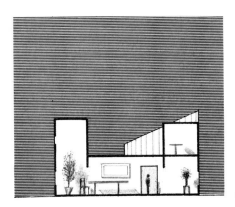

15

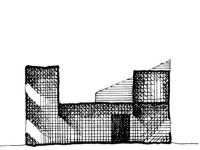

16

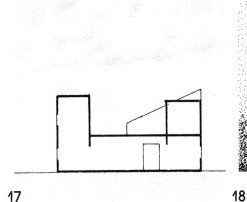

17

18

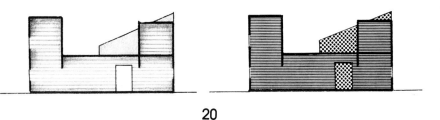

19

20

DRAWING VARIATIONS

The character of a section changes with the line, textures, and entourage. Throughout this group of drawings, the building remains the same; the background, foreground, shadows, and glass treatment change.

1. Small perspective

2. Straightedge ink drawing

3. Straightedge ink drawing, pencil background

4. Freehand ink drawing

5. Freehand ink drawing, minimal interior

6. Freehand ink drawing, stipple background

7. Straightedge drawing, stipple background

8. Straightedge drawing, straightedge interior

9. Straightedge drawing, pencil interior and background.

10. Straightedge drawing, straightedge interior

11. Straightedge drawing

12. Straightedge drawing, stipple trees

13. Straightedge drawing, pencil interior

14. Freehand drawing, pencil interior

15. Straightedge drawing, Zipatone background

16. Freehand drawing and interior

17. Straightedge drawing, pencil background

18. Straightedge drawing, stipple interior and background

19. Straightedge drawing, straight-line interior

20. Straightedge drawing, Zipatone background

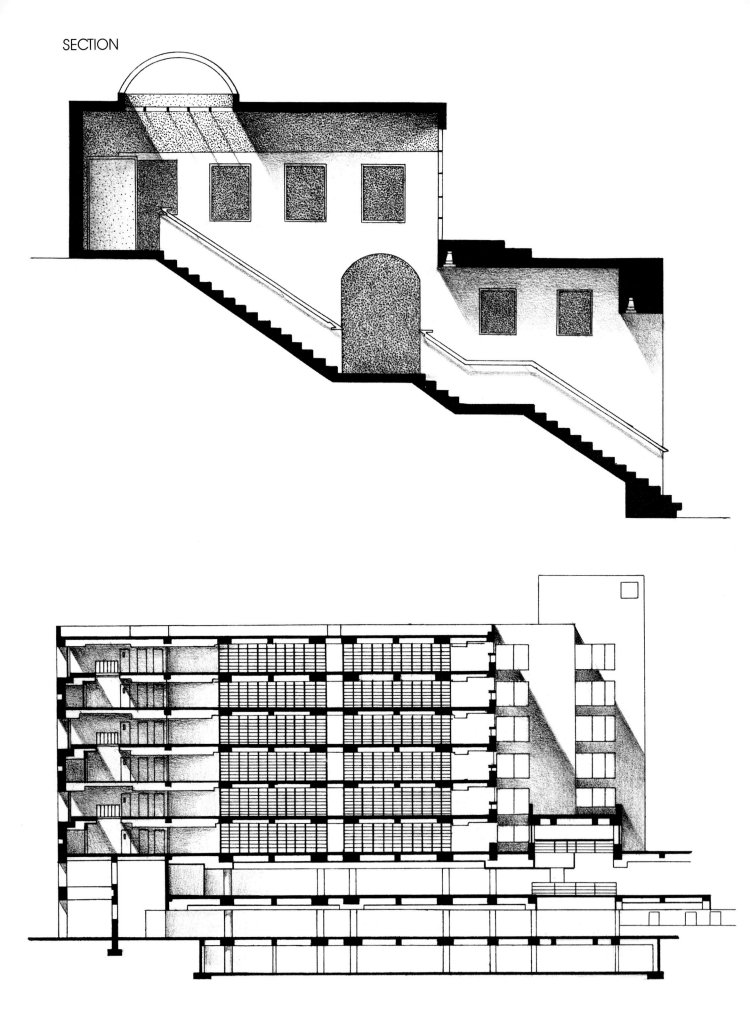

SECTION

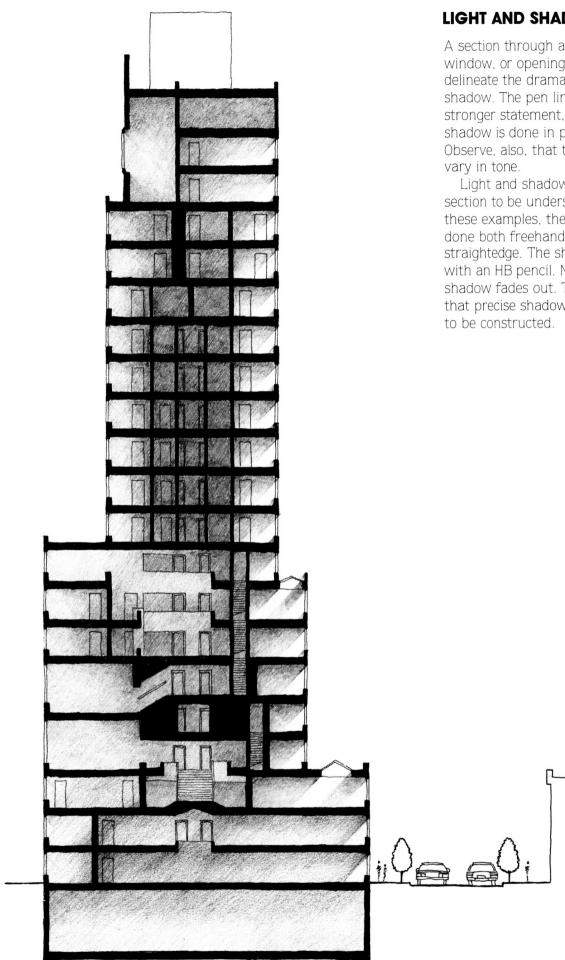

LIGHT AND SHADOW

A section through a skylight, window, or opening allows you to delineate the drama of light and shadow. The pen line is the stronger statement, while the shadow is done in pencil. Observe, also, that the shadows vary in tone.

Light and shadow allow the section to be understood. In these examples, the drawings are done both freehand and straightedge. The shadow is done with an HB pencil. Notice how the shadow fades out. This means that precise shadows do not have to be constructed.

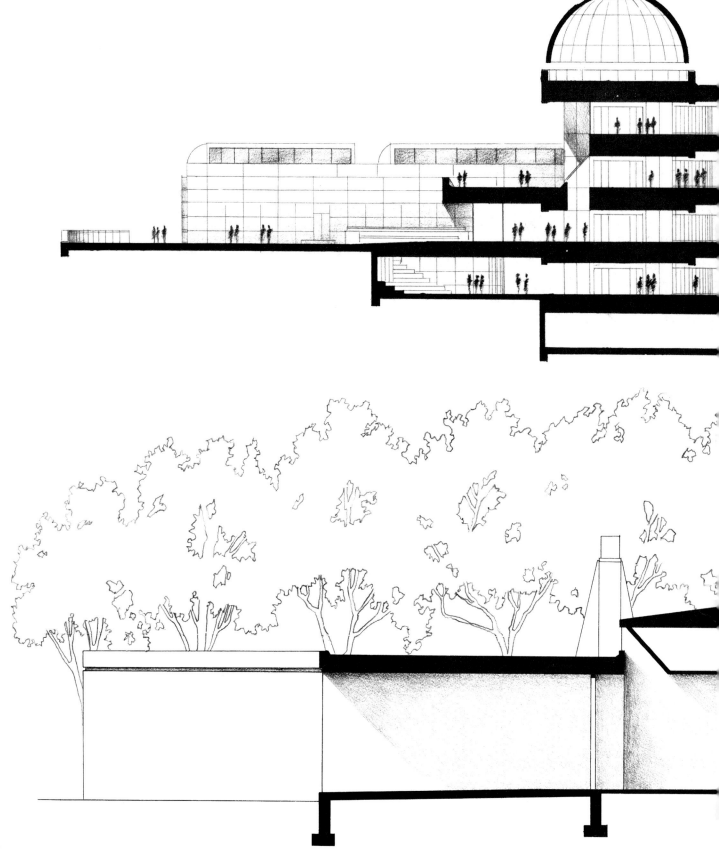

DRAMATIC EFFECT

Note the subtlety of the pencil when it appears next to the black of the ink line; also note the drama of the light as it enters the architecture.

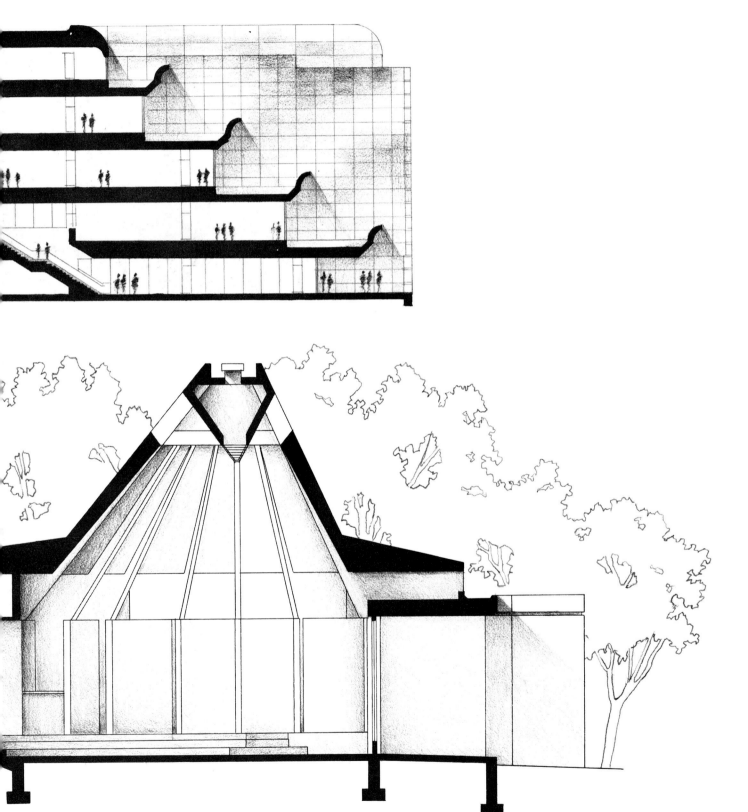

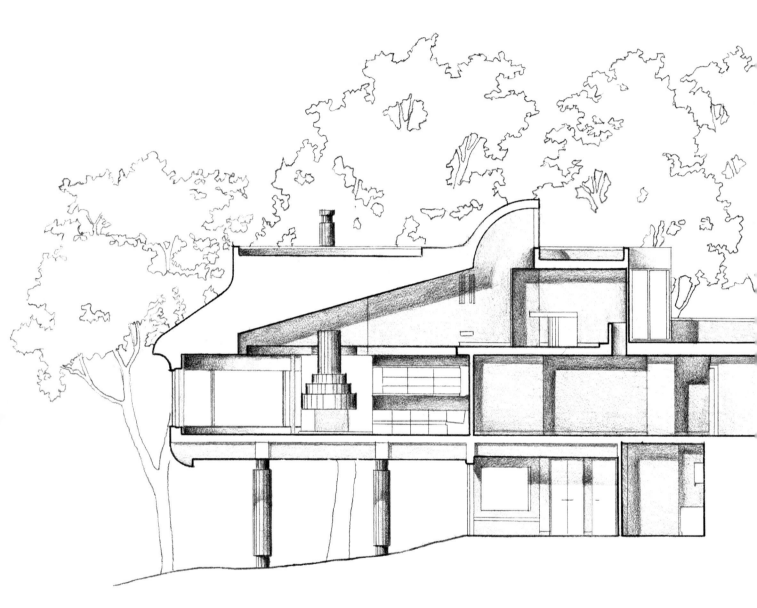

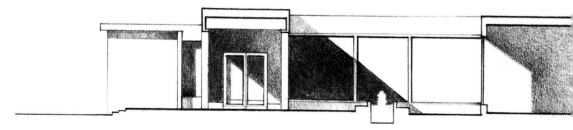

PENCIL SECTIONS

Although drawings do not have the same strength as pen and ink drawings, they do have a subtlety and a grace all their own. Pencil drawings take an overlay of texture, a blending of tones that comes only with practice.

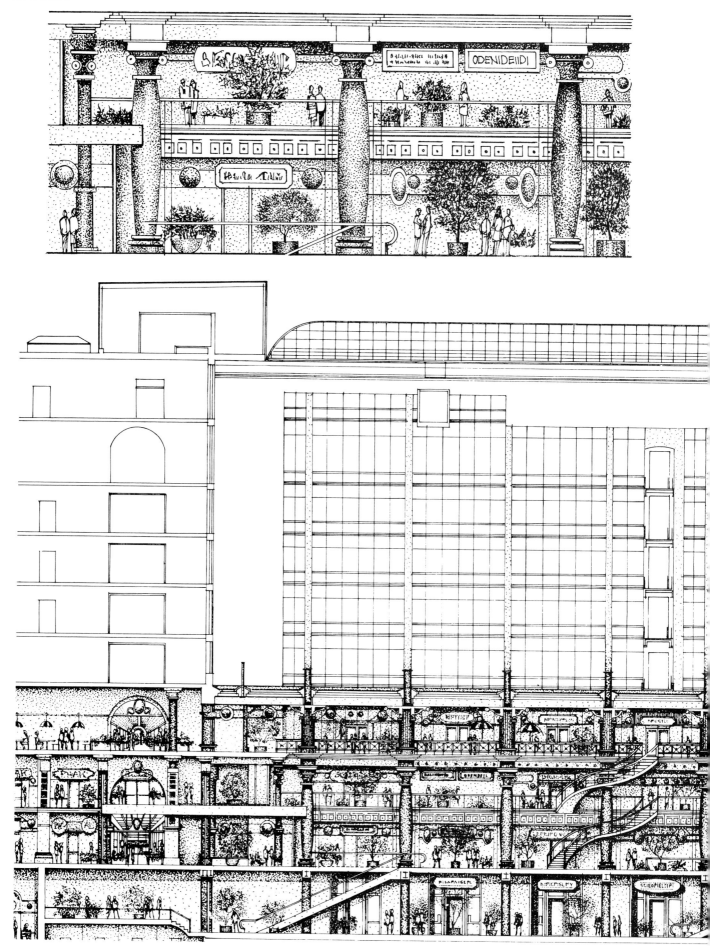

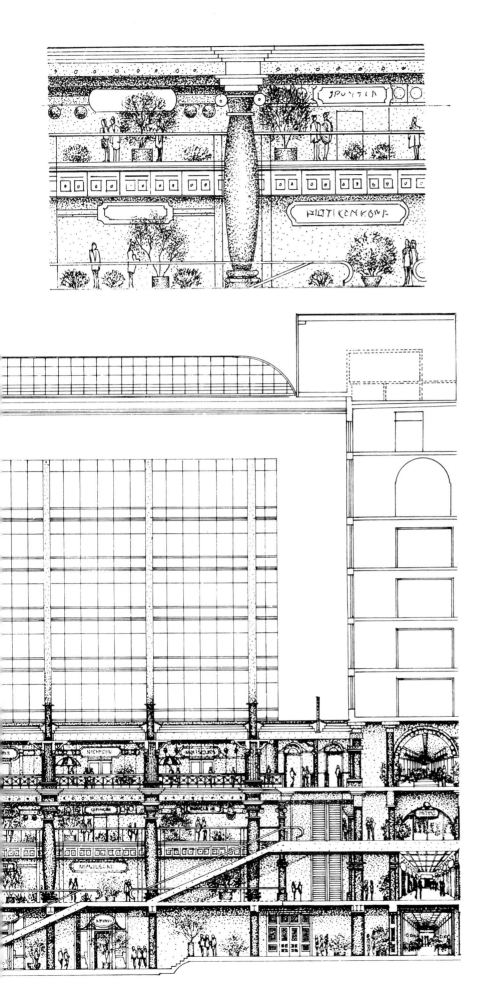

COMPLEX SECTION

A complex section, made interesting through the detail involved. Adding detail is essential because it allows us to "read" the scale of the drawing. Note the magnified details and how they make the entire drawing work.

Chapter 7: PICTORIAL

Axonometrics, plan perspectives, and section perspectives are the types of drawings that look three-dimensional. These drawings are called pictorial. A beginner should be able to draw all three pictorials—at a minimum.

Axonometric

The axonometric is a useful drawing because it is not a perspective but gives the feeling of being one.

The axonometric is drawn to any convenient architectural or metric scale. Like any type of drawing, the axonometric has positive and negative aspects. On the positive side, the drawing method is simple to understand and easy to do. The drawback of the axonometric is the viewpoint: the viewer can only look down into the space. Although informative, this is not the natural way of looking at architecture. Also, because perspective is not used at all, the drawing has a machinelike character: impersonal and a bit unreal.

One of the major reasons for drawing an axonometric is that the entire drawing is done to scale. All measurements, horizontal and vertical, are precise and easily found. Because of this accuracy, it is simple to add detail.

The axonometric is begun by arranging the plan at the angle you think will best suit your drawing. The smaller the wall angle to the horizontal, the more detail will be seen on that wall. Always test this theory of angle before you begin drawing.

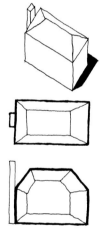

Axonometric, plan, and section

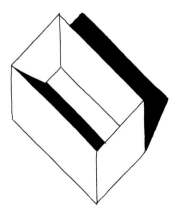

Axonometric

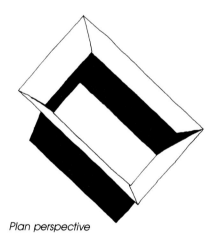

Plan perspective

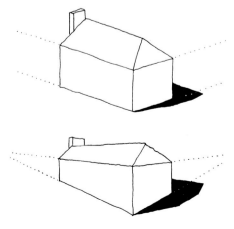

Perspective and axonometric

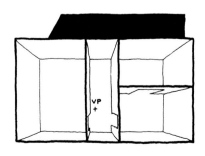

Plan perspective

Section perspective

Plan and Section Perspective

Plan and section perspectives are extremely useful because they allow the viewer to look into a space as if the roof has been lifted off (plan perspective) or as if a side wall has been cut away (section perspective).

Unlike the axonometric, in which part of two walls can be seen, all four walls can be seen in a plan perspective. Lay people usually have a difficult time understanding the meaning of floor plans and sections, but when they are shown a plan perspective or a section perspective, the space becomes clear to them.

Understanding plan and section perspective is simple. There are some very basic points to keep in mind:

Eye level. A perspective is drawn from the viewer's eye level: for example, standing on the ground, sitting in a chair, or suspended in air. Each of these locations lets the viewer see the subject from a different eye level.

The horizon. The eye level and the horizon are the same line.

Vanishing point. Railroad tracks seem to vanish to a point. This is because they are parallel lines, and in perspective, parallel lines seem to meet on the horizon at a single point, called the vanishing point.

A measuring system. In order to do a plan perspective or a section perspective, a system of measurement is needed. By building a perspective grid, you will be able to place all architectural elements easily and accurately.

Measuring

For measuring heights, you must use what is called the measuring line. In section perspective, you start with a section that is drawn to scale and then work out from that section. All heights are measured from the section, which is in scale.

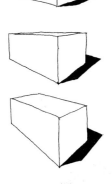

Standing, sitting, axonometric views

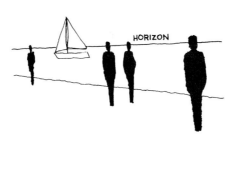

Horizon line

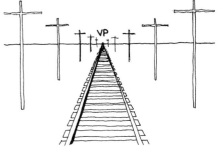

Vanishing point

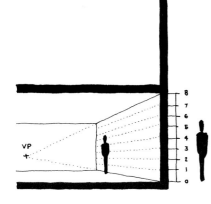

Height measurement

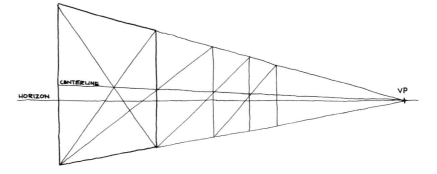

Measuring system

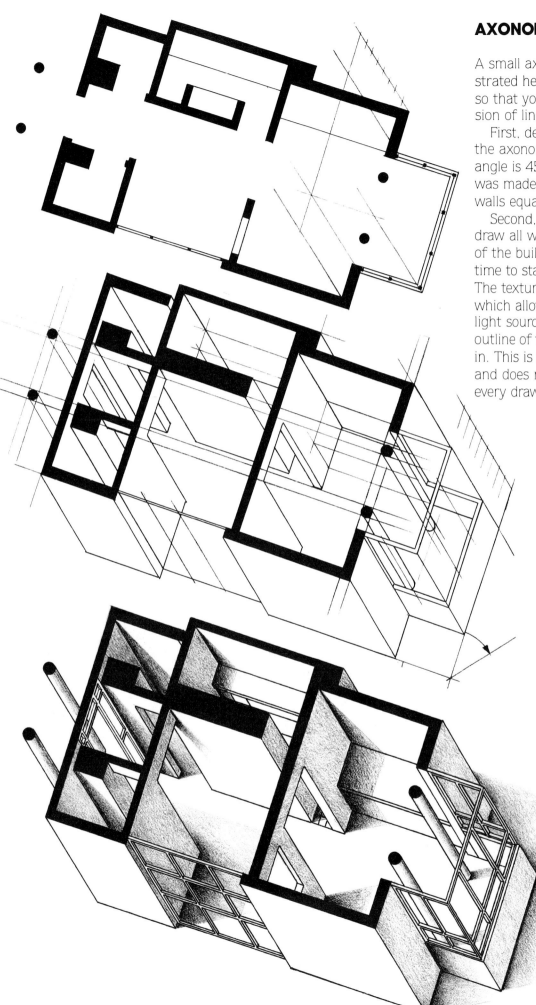

AXONOMETRIC

A small axonometric is demonstrated here, one step at a time, so that you can see the progression of lines and textures.

First, decide on the angle of the axonometric. In this case, the angle is 45 degrees. This decision was made in order to give all walls equal importance.

Second, begin to measure and draw all walls. When the outline of the building is complete, it is time to start rendering texture. The texture in this case is pencil, which allows the viewer to see a light source. For this drawing, the outline of the interior is blackened in. This is not a rule, however, and does not have to be done for every drawing.

PICTORIAL

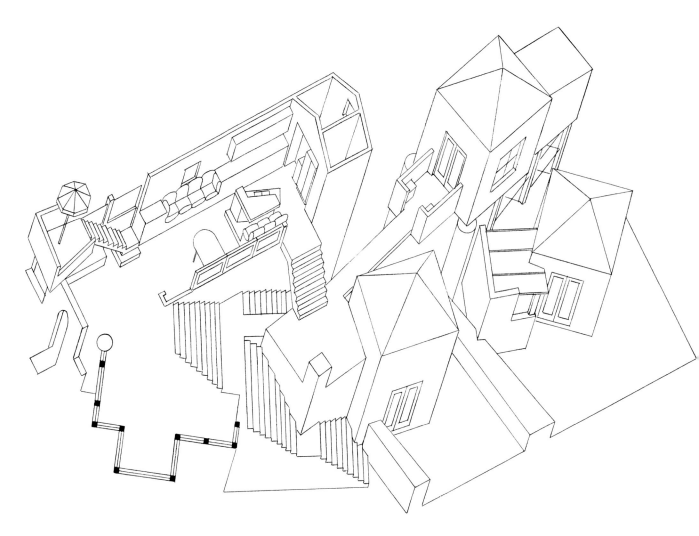

AXONOMETRIC

Here are two rather complicated architectural forms that can only be understood by using an axonometric. This type of drawing allows you to understand the volume and the changes in height more readily. The shading is done with pencil and the line work is done with pen and ink.

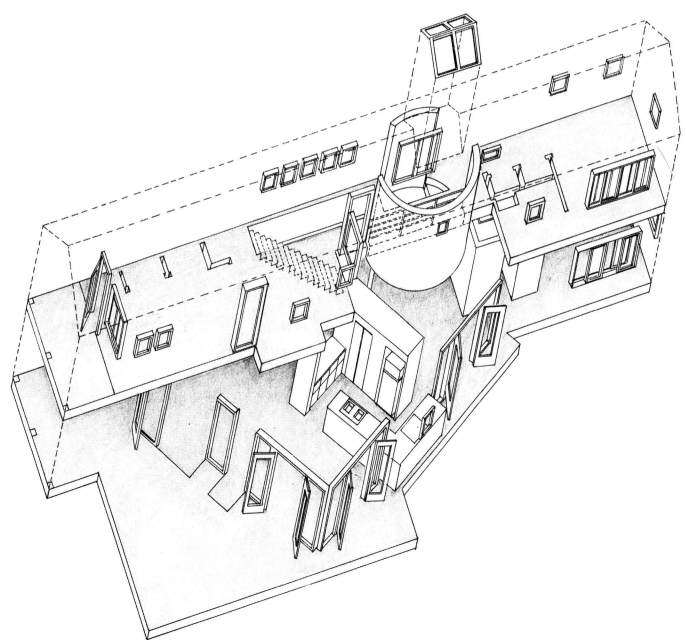

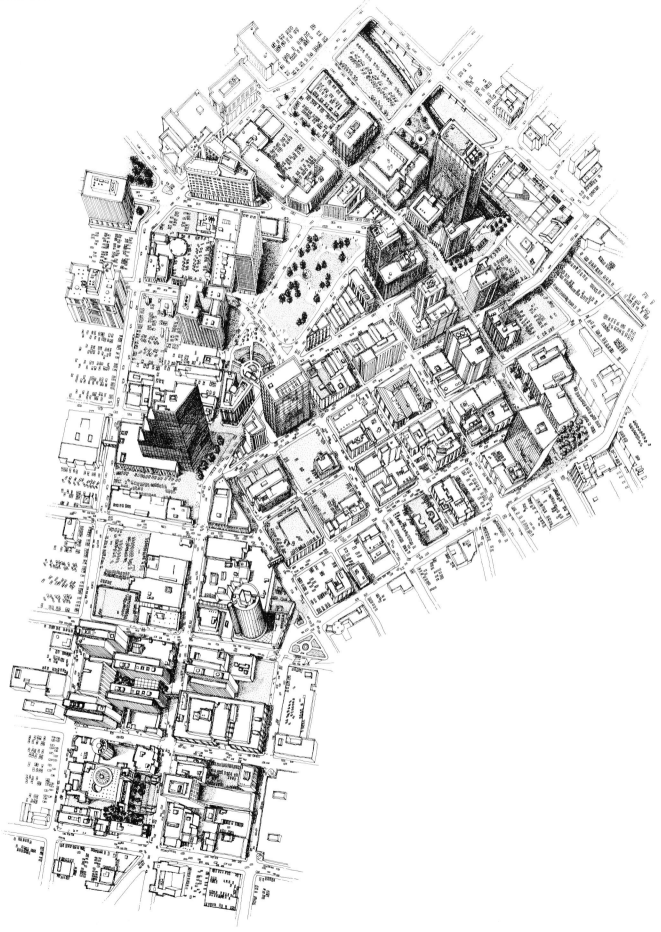

AXONOMETRIC OVERVIEW

Here is a very precise drawing of the city of Atlanta. The idea, when doing a drawing as complex as this one, is to make sure that the smallest component of the entire drawing (see sample detail) is done with great care and accuracy. In this way the entire drawing is made up of strong ingredients.

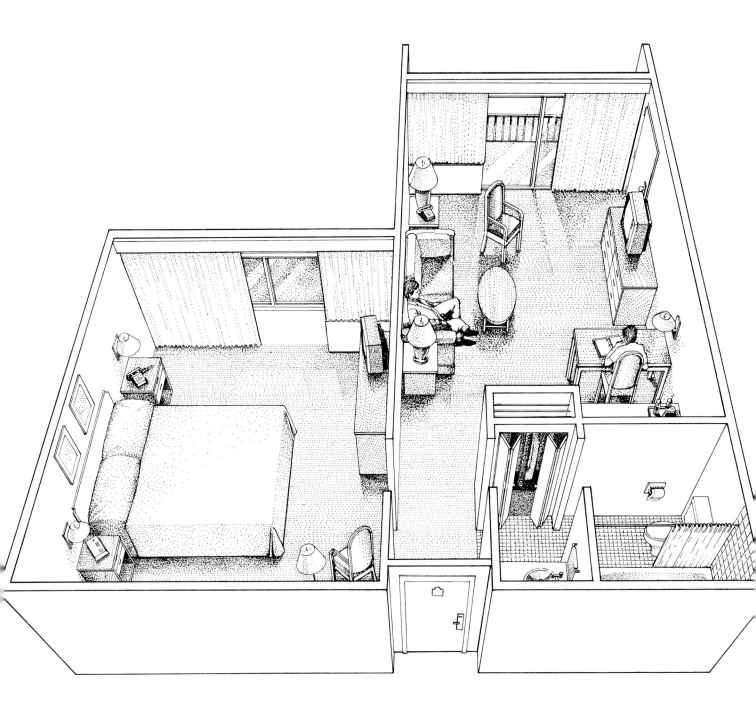

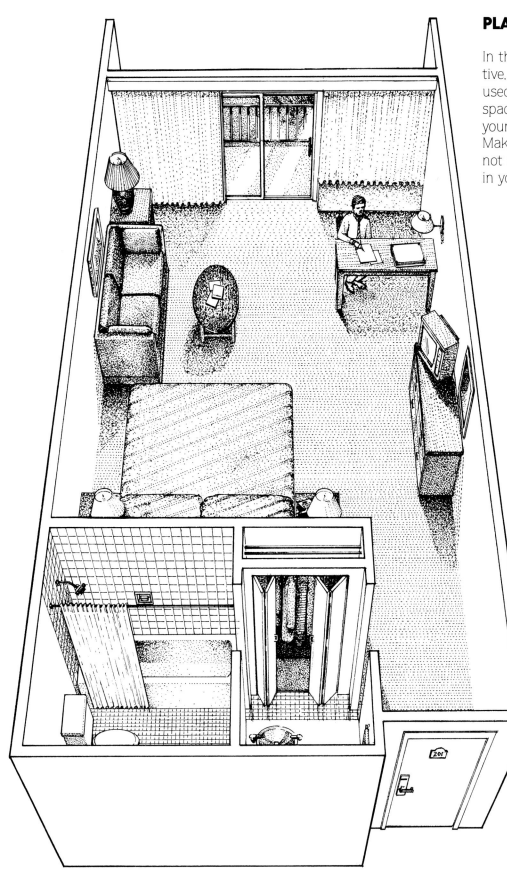

PLAN PERSPECTIVE

In this straightedge plan perspective, careful ink textures were used to delineate and explain the space. Do not overdo textures, or your drawing will get too busy. Make sure that the people are not obtrusive; remember, they are in your illustration for scale only.

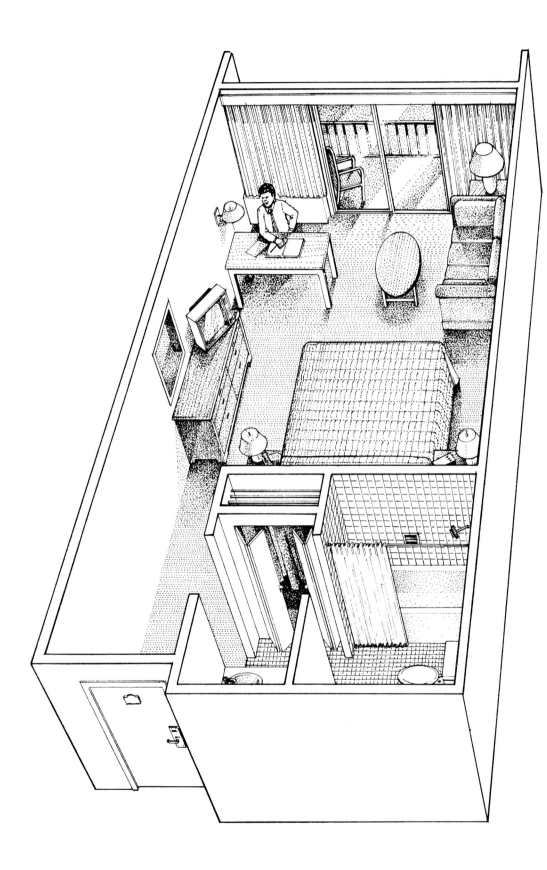

PLAN PERSPECTIVE

These are two plan perspectives that are rather simple, yet they give a very clear picture of the interior of the space. Presented to a client, these drawings would be much better selling tools than, say, floor plans and sections, because they are more easily understood. As you can see, the layout uses a simple grid method. The floor plan is then superimposed on this grid. Once the grid has been drawn, the details are projected upward, with the walls used as a measuring line.

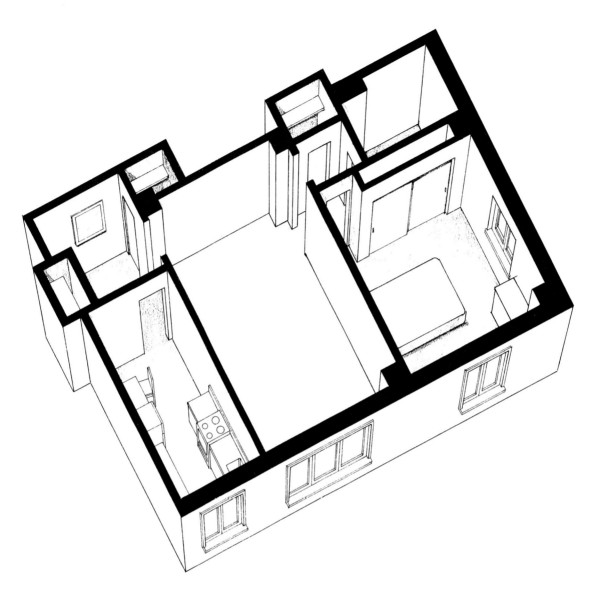

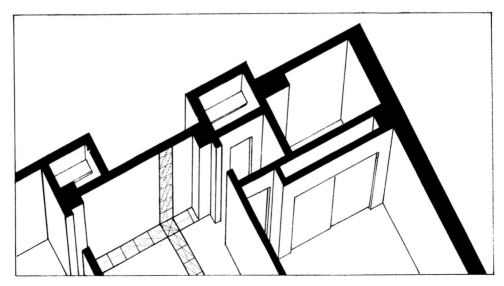

Squares used in measuring

The plans on the left were made using the square grid construction method explained on pages 108 and 109.

On the right, textures were used to create a subtle sense of enclosure and to precisely delineate materials.

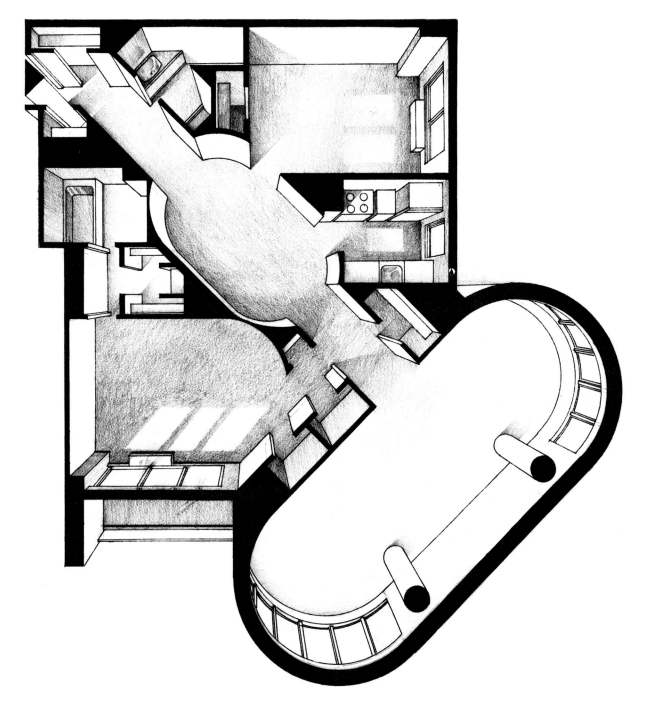

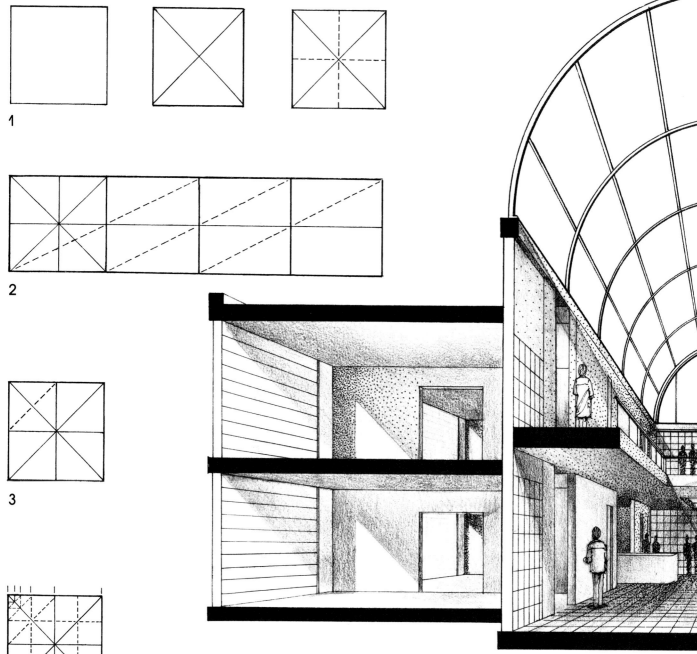

1

2

3

4

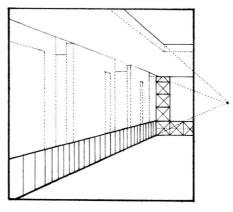

5

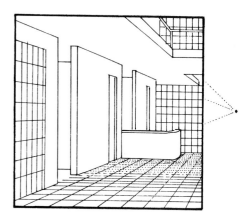

6

The drama of the space is heightened by pencil textures, which strengthen the entering light. Because a pencil line is weaker than an ink line, you can place the pencil textures right over the ink lines. The method of construction utilizes the overlay of a square grid. Follow the method shown here in diagrams 1–7 and you should have absolutely no problems.

7

SECTION PERSPECTIVE

Texture and detail are what make this drawing work. Try to move the viewer's eye around and through your space. The furniture and the textures must be in scale with one another and with the architecture.

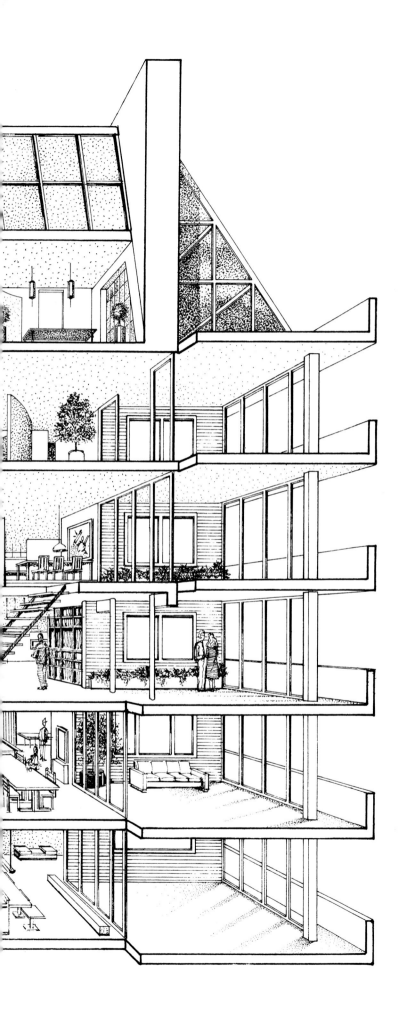

SECTION PERSPECTIVE

Another section perspective. As you can see, detail is once again the hallmark of this drawing. Be precise and careful with all the ingredients of your drawing.

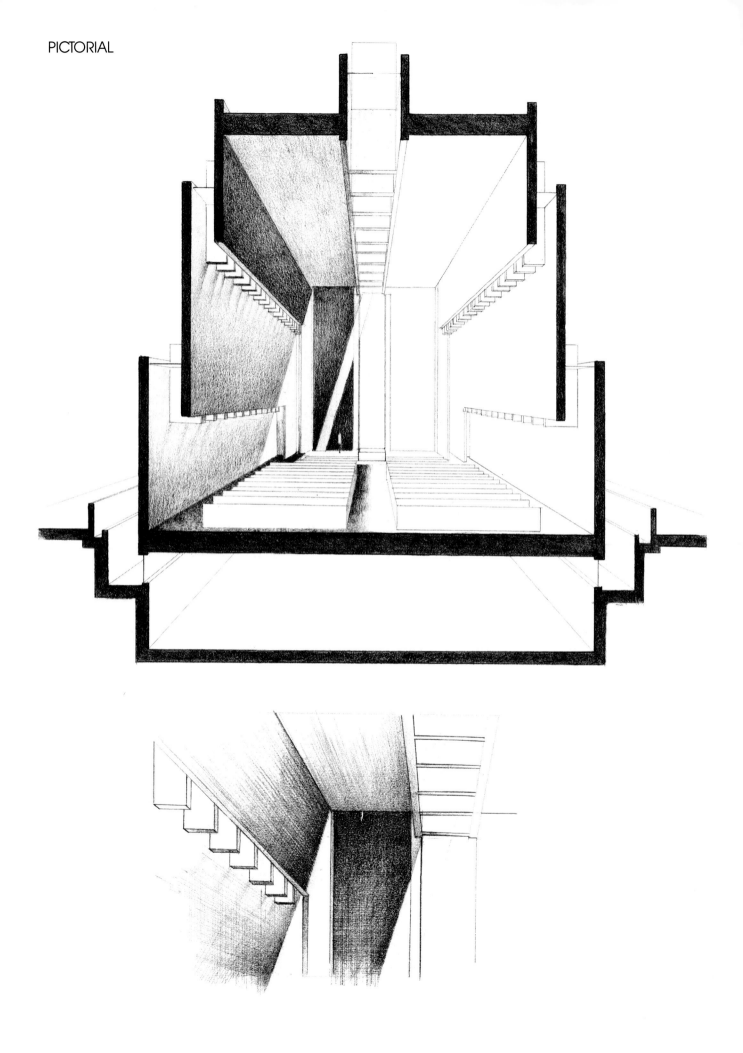

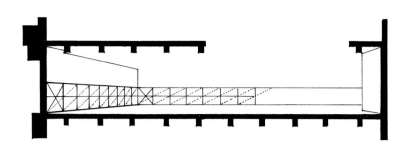

SECTION PERSPECTIVES

The rather simple section perspectives on the left use light to delineate the space. The texture that delineates the light is done with pencil. Note the simple method of layout on the right, again with the square used to create a grid system.

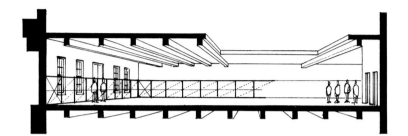

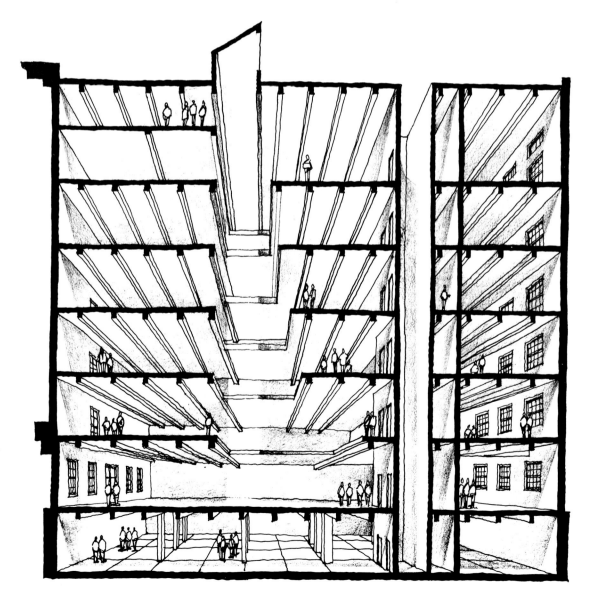

Chapter 8: OVERVIEW

Continents, states, cities, sections of cities, and large-scale projects are several examples of subjects that must be drawn from an aerial viewpoint in order to be seen in their entirety. Imagine trying to show all or even a section of New York City from an eye level of six feet. It would be absolutely impossible. Therefore, you must choose an eye level that enables you to see all that you need to see. In these cases, that eye level will necessarily be an aerial or bird's-eye view.

Having chosen the view, you will then need to decide upon your method of attack. How are you going to draw the subject? Should you work from photographs? Should you work from slides? Should you construct a grid and build your drawing within the grid? What physical character will the drawing have?

Once you have chosen the method and type of drawing you wish to draw, you are ready to do the layout. When the detailed layout has been completed and checked, you are almost ready to begin the finished drawing, but several more decisions must be made. What media are you going to utilize? What surface should you draw on? What size should the final drawing be? The answers to these questions will be based on the time available to complete the drawing and the physical character that you have determined the drawing should have. To see how these decisions are made, look at the examples on the following pages and the detailed descriptions of how they were completed.

Overview

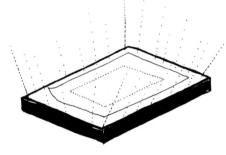

Working from photostats

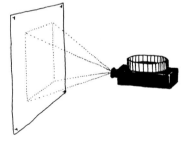

Working from slides

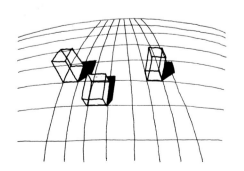

Drawing a grid

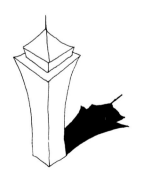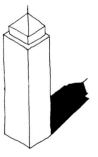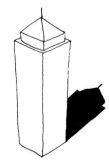

Drawing character

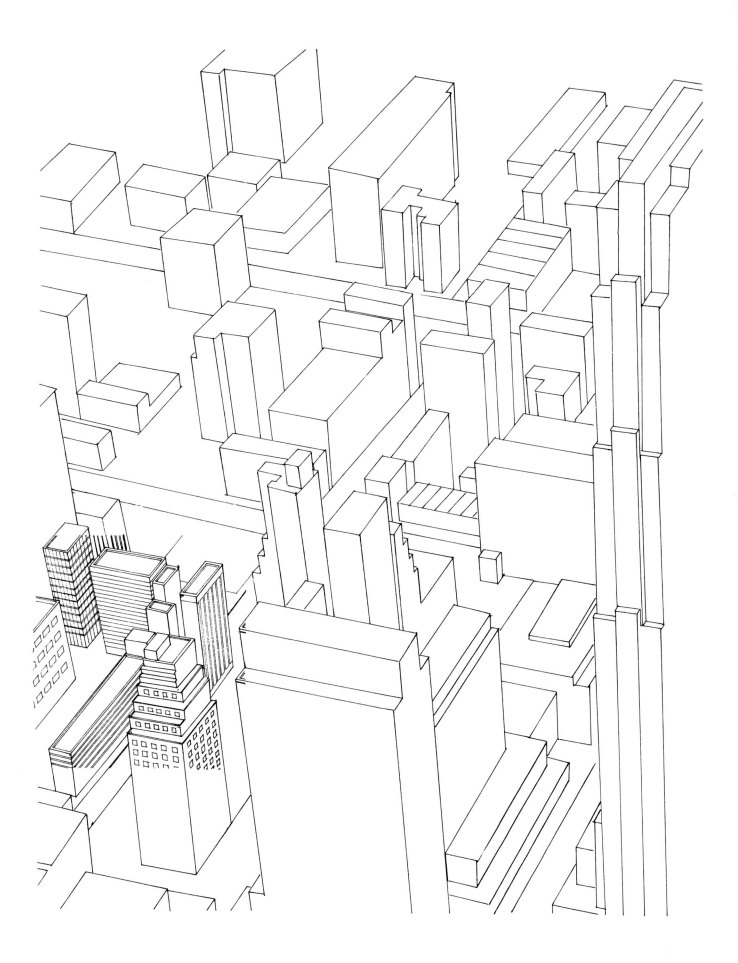

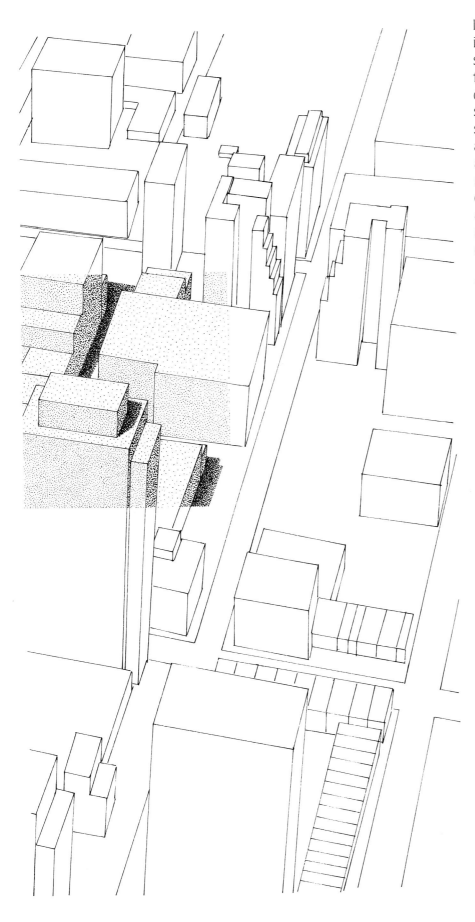

CITYSCAPE

In this overview, done at approximately a 70-degree angle to the surface, we can see about a fifteen-square-block area of the city. The larger the angle with the surface, the more that can be seen. As we look directly down, at a 90-degree angle, we see less and less of each building facade and more and more of the roofs of the buildings. In order to make an overview informative, the angle must allow us to see not only surroundings but also building facades and details of the buildings. An angle of between 55 and 70 degrees usually works best. (In drawing, as in any other discipline, a rule is not meant to be followed blindly. Different problems require different solutions.)

As you can see, the drawing is blocked in and then drawn using a straightedge. Once this has been done, the face of each building is sketched in over a grid. The whole drawing is completed in detail, in pencil. Only after all details have been checked is the final inking begun.

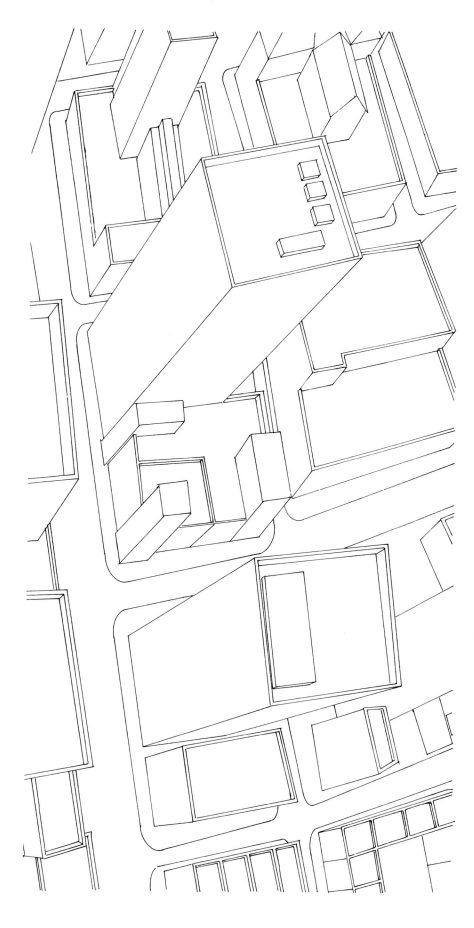

URBAN OVERVIEW

An overview done at an angle of 80 degrees does not allow us to see much of the facades of the buildings because the angle is so severe. In this drawing we are able to see the surface of the street. As a result, this drawing lends itself to use as a map or as a directional tool. The question, then, is why not just use a map? The answer is simple: a map does not have the interest, the volume, or the scale that this drawing has. In addition, a map is flat and lifeless, totally without personality or fantasy. On the other hand, a viewer can place himself or herself within this drawing and more easily understand locations and scale.

As with any pen and ink drawing, the drawing is first completed in pencil using a straightedge. The detail is added in pencil, and only then in pen and ink. The procedure is as follows: decide on a slide or a photograph as reference; draw the layout in pencil, using a straightedge, on Albanene tracing paper; verify all details; place two-ply Bristol board over the pencil layout on top of a light table; and trace the pencil layout with ink, freehand.

MANHATTAN

This drawing was done at an angle of 70 degrees with the surface of the earth, creating the curved horizon. The entire drawing was done first in pencil, with a straightedge. When all details had been added, all locations and buildings had been checked, the drawing was ready for ink. The entire drawing was inked freehand over the straightedge pencil drawing. Following the usual procedure, the underdrawing (pencil straightedge) was done on Albanene tracing paper, using a 2H pencil. The underdrawing was done on two-ply Bristol board, medium-tooth surface, with no. 000 and 0000 pens. The ink drawing took twenty-five to thirty hours to complete.

Because of the scale of the area to be drawn and the time allowed to do the drawing, minimum amounts of shading were used. The drawing is, basically, a pure line drawing. There are, however, a few small spots where texture and shading come into play. In the distance, architecture and detail fade to nothingness as the line work changes to series of dots; the space between the dots increases, and finally there is nothing. This gives the feeling of distance as the drawing recedes. The trees and grass in the foreground are also composed of dots, or stippling, as are the reflections in the water and the wake of the boats.

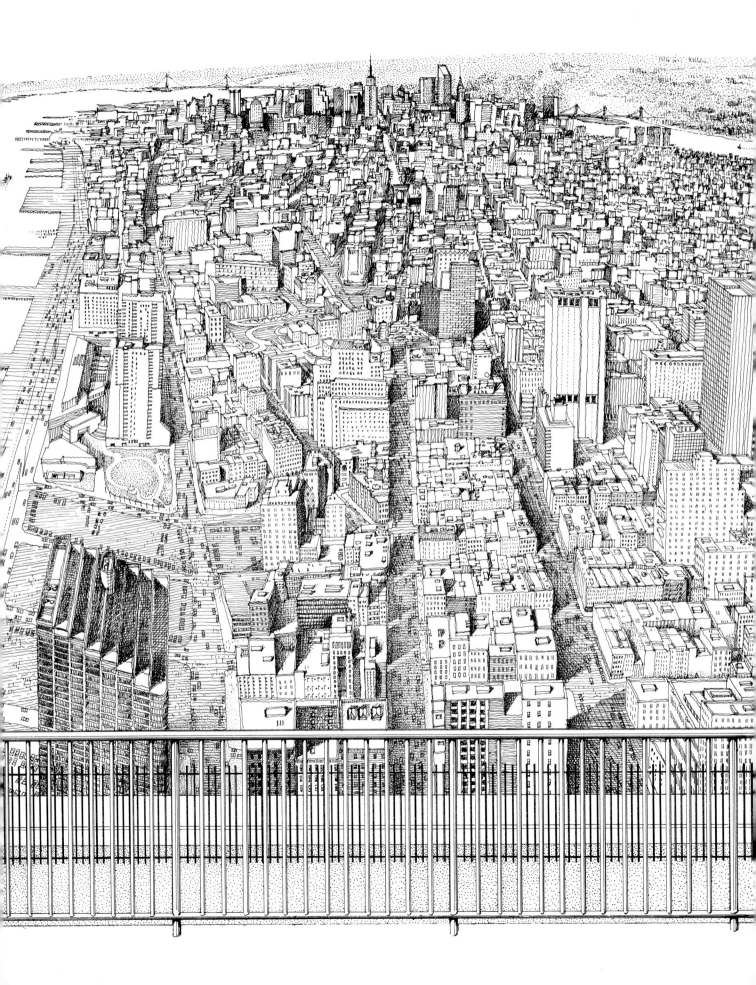

WORLD TRADE CENTER VIEW

Since this drawing was to be used in a newspaper, in which the shading of halftones such as a watercolor wash, a pencil tone, or ink marker would not reproduce well, ink line was chosen as the finished medium. A series of photographs taken from the World Trade Center was the base for the drawing. However, this presented several difficulties: when the drawing was put together, the distortion was so exaggerated that something had to be altered in order to eliminate it. Moreover, there was too much architecture to fit into the area; some buildings had to be removed in a way that no one would notice.

Once this was done, the layout was drawn on Albanene tracing paper and the final drawing begun. The finished layout was done freehand with no. 000 and 0000 technical pens.

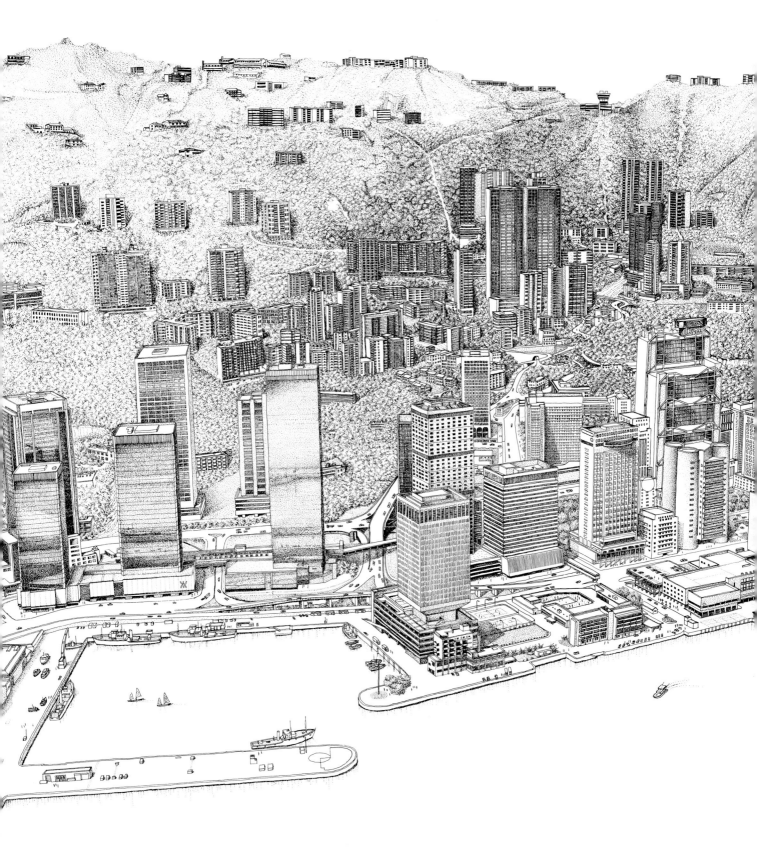

HONG KONG

The layout of this drawing was done using four overlapping photographs made with a wide-angle lens. There is less distortion of the architecture if photographs are taken in a series and then put together to form a panoramic view of a city.

Once the layout was done in pencil, it was transferred to a piece of two-ply Bristol board on a light table (the thickest board that you can still see through). The reason for working on the heaviest transparent surface is the need for erasing without tearing the surface. A good electric eraser and ink eraser can take any line or series of lines out of any drawing if it is on the proper board. Erasing does, of course, mar the surface slightly, but as long as it is not too deep, you should be able to draw right over the erasure without a problem.

As you can see, the textures were done using a combination of stippling and line work. Since the drawing was very complex, it was important that there be an order in its completion once the final inking stage was begun. First, all the buildings were outlined carefully using a freehand ink line and a technical pen. Next, all the cars, people, and boats were drawn. The trees and rocks were then stippled in. The last part drawn was the shadow and reflection of the buildings on each other and the surroundings. It is very important to have a system and to follow it, since it leads to an even, consistent drawing.

LONDON

The layout was done using two overlapping photographs. The line work was done using no. 000 and 0000 technical pens. So that the background would fade toward the horizon, the line work and stippling had to become less dense as the distance from the viewer increased. To give a sense of distance in any overview, you must use a thinner line and less detail.

As with any drawing of this scope, time is a very important element, a variable that must be estimated with precision. This drawing took approximately 250 hours to complete. The area of the drawing is thirty inches by forty inches, or twelve hundred square inches. This means it took approximately fifteen minutes drawing time per square inch. This is a good method for estimating the time required for almost any drawing. Remember, though, no method is foolproof. Some drawings might take less time because they require less detail, while others will take more time because you are using color or some other time-consuming technique.

CHICAGO

This drawing of Chicago and the countryside surrounding it was done for a poster. It retains a certain amount of realism yet is a cartoon in the sense that the buildings and landscape are not precisely accurate. The geography, while giving the feel of Chicago, is not topographically correct. It is important when doing a drawing of this type to keep the integrity of the city. This means that the locations and relationships of buildings and neighborhoods should approximate reality. This allows the viewer to recognize and find specific buildings while understanding that the drawing is not *totally* accurate. In any drawing of an architectural character, geography, scale, and direction play an important part in making the drawing understandable.

The drawing was done using no. 000 and 0000 technical pens.

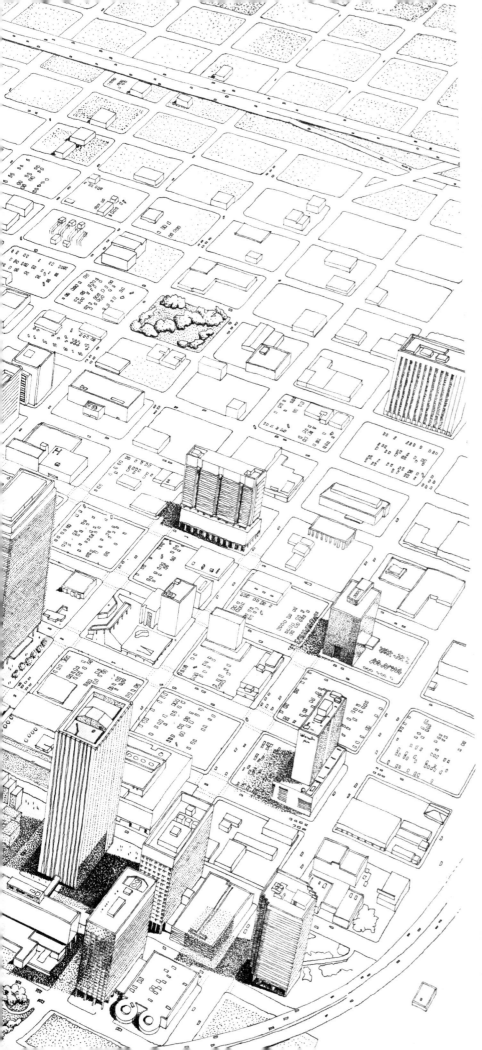

HOUSTON

This was a much more complex and time-consuming drawing than the preceding overviews. The major problem to overcome in completing this drawing was that many of the major buildings had not yet been built. Architectural drawings had to be interpreted and the proposed buildings injected into the existing landscape of Houston, using a photograph as a grid. Making all this input work together in the same scale and remain visually understandable was accomplished by the following steps:

1. A grid was created within the existing photograph. The photograph gave accurate measurements for this grid.

2. The new buildings were placed within the grid, first in rough form. Then the architecture and the line were refined.

3. When the accuracy of the work was satisfactory, the final inking was done.

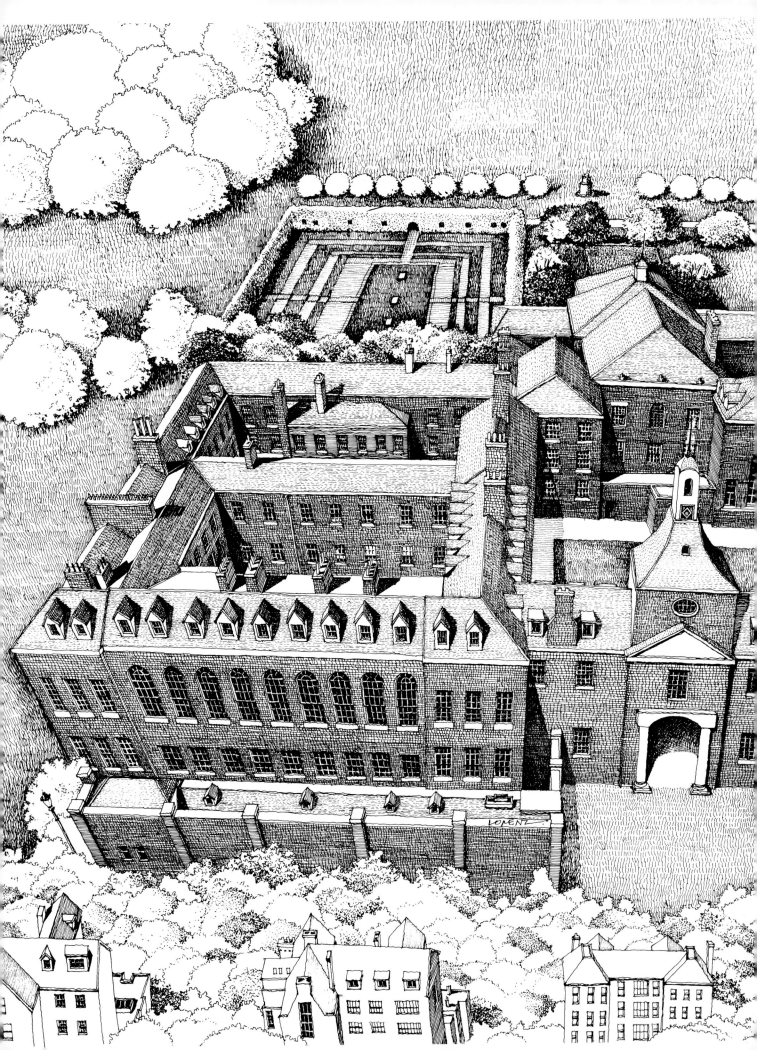

KENSINGTON PALACE

This drawing was done by working from photographs of the castle and then transcribing them to a grid that was drawn specifically for the job. To give the building a more dynamic look, a vanishing point was established below it. This allows the building to soar off the page. This drawing was done freehand using no. 00 and 000 technical pens. The textures of the brick and the grass are what give it solidity and character.

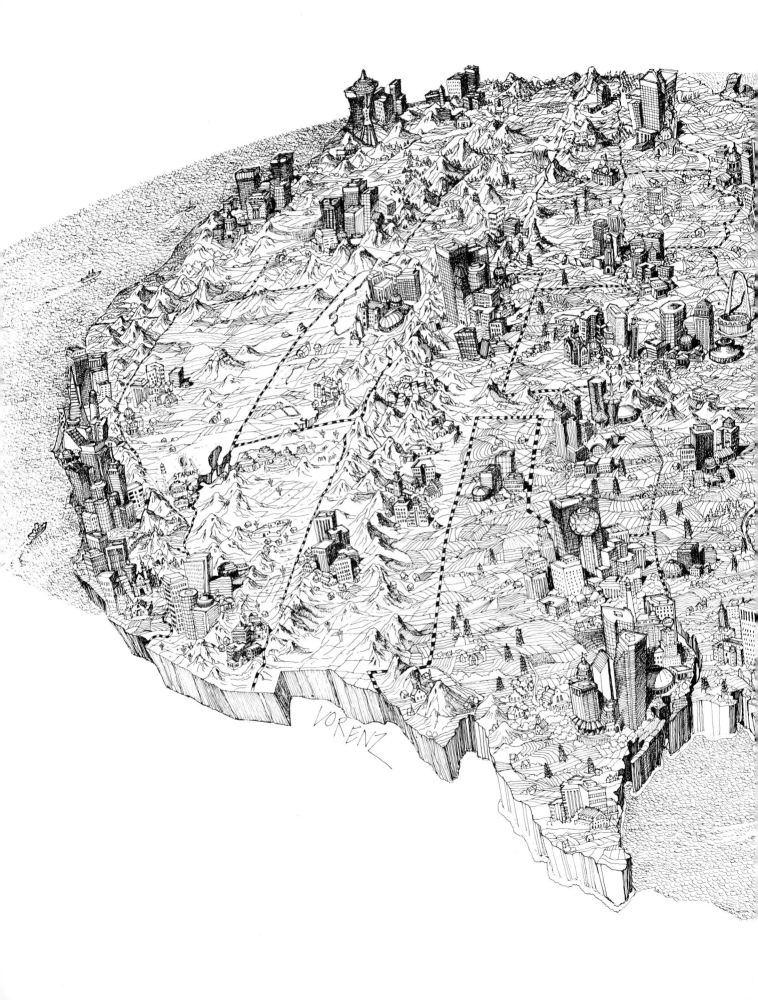

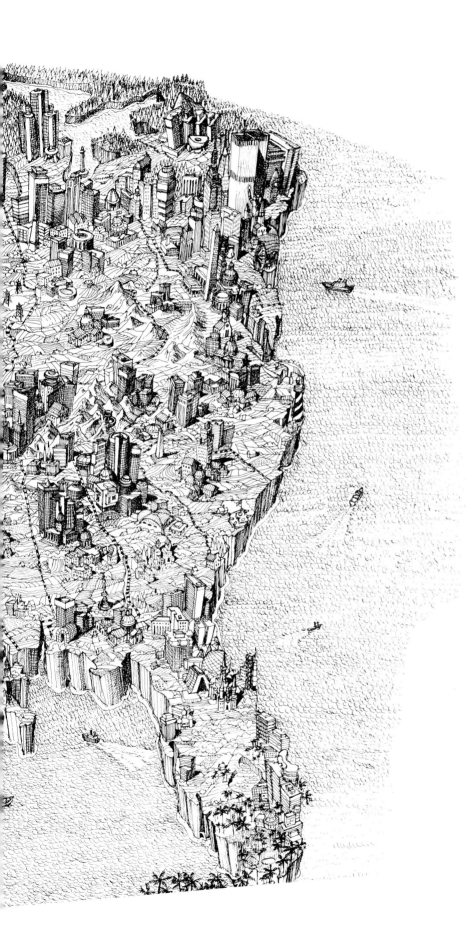

MAP OF THE UNITED STATES

This drawing was created as a humorous approach to the idea of a map. The layout was done over a curved grid in two steps. First, the state borders and city locations were drawn in pencil. Second, the cities were located and drawn, still in pencil. As you can see, the buildings and the landscape help to create the drawing's scale. While the scale is not totally accurate, it creates a visual understanding of the architectural and natural relationships.

This understanding is a visual one. It is a quality that comes to your drawing through experience and self-evaluation. You must be constantly critical of your own work. You must establish a picture in your mind of what your drawing should look like when it is finished. Once this mental image is established, never be satisfied until your drawing matches it. This drawing was done entirely freehand using no. 000 and 0000 technical pens. It took approximately 100 hours to complete.

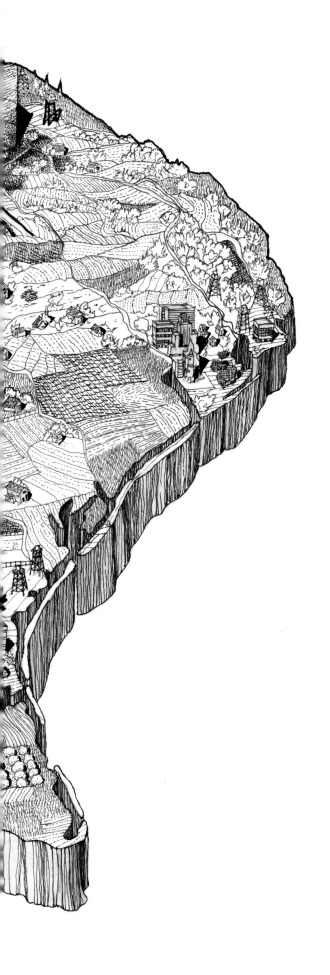

MAP OF TEXAS

The same method of drawing was applied to this as to the previous overview of the United States. A series of visual examples makes clear the progression from pencil outline to textures to landscapes to the final shading.

INDEX

This book was prepared by Read/Write Press of Princeton.
New Jersey for the Whitney Library of Design.

Read/Write Press
Project Manager: Dorothy Spencer
Editor: Virginia Croft
Design/Mechanicals: Jennifer Place

Whitney Library of Design
Acquisition Editor: Julia Moore
Editor: Cornelia Guest
Production Manager: Ellen Greene
Jacket Designer: Bob Fillie

Set in 11-point Quorum Light and Avant Garde Bold